Nine Untold Truths About Heart's Intelligence

Unlocking The Wisdom Within

Dedication

I dedicate this book to my Pappaji (my father-in-law), who has been a pillar of support in my life. Thirty years ago, he read my palms and said, "You are going to write a book." I didn't fully grasp the depth of his words at that time, but today, as I bring this book to life, I realize the power of his vision and belief in me. His encouragement, wisdom, and faith in my journey have been a guiding light, and for that, I am forever grateful.

I also dedicate this book to Mummyji (my mother-in-law), whose love for writing Gujarati fiction stories has always inspired me. She had a beautiful way of weaving words into emotions, and as I write these pages, I feel deeply connected to her creative spirit. Her passion for storytelling lives on, and I honor her legacy through this work of writing.

Purpose of writing this book

Nine untold truths about Heart's
Intelligence – Unlocking hearts wisdom

Purpose of Writing This Book: "Nine Untold
Truths About Heart's Intelligence –
Unlocking Heart's Wisdom"

The purpose of writing this book is to share
with you the transformative power of the
heart's intelligence and its profound ability
to guide us through life's challenges. In our
fast-paced, mind-driven world, we often
neglect the deep wisdom our heart holds,
yet it is the heart that has the key to true
fulfillment, emotional healing, and purpose.

Through this book, I aim to reveal the nine
untold truths about the heart's intelligence,
helping you understand how this wisdom
can unlock your potential and create a life
of peace, love, and personal growth. Each
truth offers insight into how the heart's
intelligence plays a crucial role in our
emotional well-being, decision-making,
relationships, and healing.

By tapping into the heart's innate power, we can transcend fear, doubt, and emotional blocks, paving the way for greater self-awareness and authenticity. Through this exploration, I invite you to connect deeply with your heart's wisdom, embracing its guidance to make empowered choices and heal from past wounds.

This book isn't just a collection of concepts—it's an invitation to embark on a journey of emotional and spiritual healing, reconnecting with the most important part of your being: your heart. May these pages inspire you to live a life filled with love, clarity, and alignment with your true purpose.

In this book, I have also provided tools, exercises, and affirmations to help you practically apply the wisdom of the heart's intelligence in your daily life. These tools are designed to support you in shifting your mindset, healing emotional wounds, and cultivating a deeper connection with your heart's wisdom.

The exercises are crafted to guide you through self-reflection and action steps that promote healing and personal growth. Each exercise is a simple yet powerful way to realign yourself with your true essence and strengthen your heart's connection to your mind, body, and soul.

The affirmations offered throughout the book are empowering statements that you can incorporate into your daily routine. They are designed to reinforce positive beliefs and strengthen the energy of love, self-acceptance, and inner peace. By repeating these affirmations, you will start to create new, supportive thought patterns that align with your heart's highest potential.

Together, these tools, exercises, and affirmations will help you unlock the transformative power of your heart and lead you toward a life of fulfillment, healing, and alignment with your true purpose.

Preface

In a world that often values logic over emotion, speed over stillness, and doing over being, many of us have lost touch with the deepest wisdom that resides within: the wisdom of the heart. For years, I lived life trying to meet external expectations, driven by the need to please others and avoid conflict. I ignored the whispers of my heart, believing that success and happiness were to be found outside of me. But in doing so, I lost myself. It wasn't until I began to reconnect with my heart's intelligence that I found the clarity and peace I had been seeking. The heart holds profound wisdom—guiding us through life's challenges, offering insights that transcend logic, and leading us back to our truest selves. It is through understanding and embracing this intelligence that we can unlock our potential, heal old wounds, and create lives that are authentic and fulfilling.

In this book, I will share the nine untold truths about the heart's intelligence. These truths have been revealed to me through my journey of healing and self-discovery.

They have guided me, and they will guide you too, if you are ready to listen. Each chapter is an invitation to explore the depths of your heart, to heal, and to transform. It is my deepest hope that this book will help you reconnect with your heart's wisdom and empower you to live a life that is aligned with your soul's deepest desires.

Forward

We often look outside of ourselves for answers—seeking guidance in books, mentors, masters, gurus, or systems of thought. But the most profound source of wisdom lies within each of us. The heart, which has been overlooked and underestimated in many areas of life, is the true seat of wisdom. When we begin to listen to its whispers, rather than drown them out with the noise of the mind, we unlock the infinite potential within. The journey to accessing your heart's intelligence is not about gaining new information, but about remembering what has always been inside of you. It's about shedding the layers of conditioning, fear, and self-doubt that have kept you from living authentically. It's about learning to trust the wisdom that flows from your heart, which has been guiding you all along. Through my own experiences as a healer, coach, and spiritual seeker, I have witnessed the transformational power of reconnecting with the heart. It has the ability to guide us through difficult decisions, heal emotional wounds, and lead us to a life of purpose and fulfillment. In this book, I share nine untold truths about the heart's intelligence—truths that I've learned through both my own journey and the experiences of those I've had the privilege of guiding. As you read these pages, I encourage you to approach them with an open heart. Allow yourself to connect with the wisdom that is already within you. Your heart is calling you to listen. Will you answer? May this book inspire you to step into your own heart's wisdom and transform your life in ways you never imagined.

A Note to the Reader

As you read through the pages of this book, you may find yourself encountering many questions that serve as gentle nudges. These questions are designed to invite your heart to speak to you. They may spark a deep sense of awareness, opening doors to insights you've been longing to hear. My invitation to you is simple: this book may be short, but it holds immense value. Keep your pen and journal ready, for your heart's intelligence might want to communicate with you. Take a moment to pause, reflect, and write down the thoughts, emotions, or realizations that arise. This is not just a journey through my words, but an exploration of your own heart's wisdom. Trust the process, and let your heart guide you. I am truly excited for you to embark on this transformative journey.

Acknowledgments

This book is not just the result of my efforts but also of the unwavering support and encouragement I received from my loved ones.

I sincerely acknowledge my husband and son, whose constant encouragement and belief in me kept me motivated throughout this journey. Their patience, love, and unwavering support gave me the strength to bring my thoughts and experiences to life on these pages.

I also extend my heartfelt gratitude to Jatin, who inspired me to think about the book cover and title long before I even began writing. His vision and insight planted the seeds for this book, and I am truly grateful for his creative influence in shaping its identity.

A special thank you to all the wonderful souls who encouraged me by pre-ordering copies of this book. Your faith in my work, even before its completion, has been deeply inspiring and motivating. Your support has strengthened my belief in this journey, and I am truly grateful for every one of you.

I am deeply grateful to my mom and dad for raising me with so much care and love. I will always be thankful for the values and *sanskaras* they have instilled in me. Your guidance and unconditional love have shaped me into who I am today.

I also acknowledge my sisters and brothers, whose presence in my life has always been a source of support and joy. Thank you for being part of this beautiful journey.

To everyone who has been a part of my journey, knowingly or unknowingly — thank you for being my guiding light.

Roop Lakhani

<u>INDEX</u>

Introduction

I know this book has been a part of my being and journey. As I look back, I realize that it was born from my life experiences— the moments that shaped me, both pleasant and unpleasant. Every challenge and event has contributed to my growth and maturity. Through these pages, I have reflected on my journey, weaving together the lessons learned and the wisdom gained. This book is not just a collection of thoughts but a manifestation of the person I have become, shaped by the twists and turns of life.

I am a heart-centric person, and I felt deeply connected to my heart's wisdom as I wrote this book. It was a journey of listening, reflecting, and pouring out the truths I have discovered. I believe there will be many takeaways for you, the reader, and I sincerely hope that these words resonate with you.

I look forward to hearing your feedback, thoughts, and comments, as they are a cherished part of this shared journey. Please feel free to connect with me at roop@tarotfuture.com. Your words of encouragement will inspire me to write more books.

The Nine Untold Truths of the Heart's Intelligence

Throughout this book, we will uncover nine untold truths about the heart—truths that have been hidden in plain sight, waiting for us to listen and reconnect. These truths will guide you on a transformative journey of understanding, healing, and empowerment. Each truth unveils a different aspect of the heart's intelligence, unlocking its immense potential to guide your life, heal your wounds, and lead you to your most authentic self.

Let's take a brief look at the nine truths you will explore:

The Heart Speaks in Silence
The heart communicates in a quiet, subtle language that goes beyond words. In this truth, we'll explore how to listen to the silent messages your heart has been sending all along and how these whispers can guide you toward your truest desires.

Pain Unlocks Its Secrets
Pain is often seen as something to avoid, but in reality, it is one of the heart's most

powerful teachers. This truth reveals how emotional and physical pain can serve as a gateway to deeper wisdom and healing.

The Heart Holds Emotional Memory & Influences Your Thoughts and Emotions
Your heart carries emotional memories from past experiences that shape your thoughts and actions. Understanding how these emotional memories influence your behavior will help you break free from old patterns and heal unresolved emotions.

Your Heart Speaks to Your Body: The Silent Language of Emotions & Health
The connection between the heart and the body is profound. This truth explores how the heart's intelligence affects your physical health and how paying attention to your body's signals can lead to deeper emotional healing.

The Heart is Connected to Your Intuition and Creativity—Your Heart Knows More Than You Think!
Your heart is a wellspring of intuition and creativity, offering insights that the mind cannot access. By reconnecting with your

heart, you unlock your intuitive abilities and creative potential, allowing you to navigate life with greater confidence.

The Heart's Intelligence Can Heal You – It Holds Infinite Wisdom
The heart is not only a source of guidance but also healing. This truth reveals how the heart can help you heal emotional wounds, release negative patterns, and create a life of peace and balance.

The Heart is the Seat of Consciousness
The heart is more than just an organ; it is the seat of consciousness, where our deepest awareness resides. This truth will help you understand how the heart is connected to your soul's journey and your highest potential.

The Heart Guides You Toward Authenticity
Authenticity is at the core of a fulfilling life. This truth reveals how the heart guides you toward living in alignment with your true self, free from external pressures and societal expectations.

The Heart Holds the Blueprint of Your Purpose

Your heart knows your life's purpose. In this final truth, we'll explore how reconnecting with your heart's wisdom can reveal your authentic path and help you live a life of fulfillment and meaning.

Role of Your Heart

Consider the connections between your emotions and your heart. How do your feelings influence your physical state? Conversely, how does your heart's condition affect your emotions? Is there a harmony to be nurtured between the two?

As you navigate the journey of life, ponder the role of your heart in fostering resilience and balance. How can you cultivate a deeper relationship with your emotional and spiritual heart? What practices might help you align your heart's rhythm with the ebb and flow of your experiences?

Isn't it fascinating that the heart is the bridge between the mind, body, and soul? We often think of the heart as just a physical organ, but have you ever wondered about its deeper role? Beyond pumping blood, could it also be the center that balances our emotions, thoughts, and spiritual energy?

Think about this: The heart chakra, or Anahata, sits right in the center of the seven chakras. It connects the lower three chakras—rooted in survival, passion, and willpower—with the upper three, which guide intuition, wisdom, and divine connection. Isn't it strange that our ability to love, forgive, and feel compassion lies at this very intersection?

Life moves in cycles of ups and downs, just like a heartbeat. If the heart stops, life ceases. If our emotional and spiritual heart shuts down, don't we feel lifeless too? When was the last time you truly listened to your heart's wisdom instead of just your mind's logic?

What if the secret to balance isn't found in extremes but in the heart's ability to merge both worlds—the physical and the spiritual, the human and the divine? Perhaps, in tuning into our heart's rhythm, we unlock the harmony we have been searching for all along.

So, I ask you—how deeply are you connected to your heart? And what might change in your life if you truly honored its wisdom?

What matters to the heart?

What matters to the heart, in the emotional and spiritual sense, is deeply intertwined with the essence of our being, guiding us toward love, connection, and truth. The heart is the seat of our deepest feelings and desires, and what matters to it reflects the fundamental aspects of life that fuel our happiness, fulfillment, and growth.

Here's what truly matters to the heart:

1. Love

Love is at the core of the heart's intelligence. It fuels everything we do, from loving ourselves to the love we give to others. Love is not just romantic—it's compassion, kindness, empathy, and unconditional acceptance. The heart thrives on love, and it deeply craves connection and bonding with others. When we honor love, we open ourselves to deeper emotional fulfillment and meaningful relationships.

◆ What to reflect on:

Do you love yourself without judgment?

How do you express love in your daily interactions?

Are you open to receiving love from others?

2. Authenticity

Living authentically is one of the most powerful ways to honor your heart. The heart wants you to show up as your true self, not pretending to be something you're not. It desires honesty, vulnerability, and the freedom to express your uniqueness without fear of judgment. When you live authentically, you feel more aligned with who you truly are, bringing peace and clarity.

◆ What to reflect on:

Are you being true to yourself in all aspects of your life?

Where are you hiding parts of yourself to fit in?

How would it feel to embrace your authentic self without fear?

3. Connection

The heart yearns for connection—deep, meaningful relationships that nourish the soul. Whether it's connecting with loved ones, nature, or even our inner selves, the heart longs for connection because it provides a sense of belonging, security, and purpose. True connection helps us feel seen, heard, and valued. It reminds us that we are not alone.

◈ What to reflect on:

Who do you feel connected to at a soul level?

Are there relationships in your life that nourish your heart?

How do you foster deeper connections with others?

4. Peace

Peace of mind is a vital need for the heart. The heart seeks calmness and tranquility, free from chaos, stress, and inner conflict. It desires emotional balance and the absence of unnecessary drama. When we are at peace, we are better able to listen to our inner wisdom and make decisions that align with our true selves.

◆ What to reflect on:

Are you at peace with yourself?

What brings you inner calm?

How can you create more peace in your life?

5. Healing

The heart is deeply involved in our healing journey. Whether it's emotional wounds, past traumas, or personal setbacks, the heart seeks to heal and grow. Healing is an essential part of our human experience, allowing us to move forward with wisdom and strength. When we honor the heart's need for healing, we open ourselves to growth, forgiveness, and transformation.

◆ What to reflect on:

Are there wounds in your heart that need healing?

What steps can you take to heal your emotional scars?

How can you be gentle with yourself during this process?

6. Courage

The heart loves courage—especially the courage to stand up for what we believe in, to face our fears, and to take risks in the pursuit of our dreams. Courage is what helps us push through obstacles, embrace challenges, and create a life that aligns with our desires. The heart doesn't fear change— it welcomes it, knowing that it leads to growth and expansion.

◆ What to reflect on:

When was the last time you stepped outside of your comfort zone?

What is one fear that you would love to overcome?

How can you summon the courage to take the next step?

7. Gratitude

Gratitude opens the heart and attracts more positivity into our lives. The heart thrives when it acknowledges the good things in life, big or small. Gratitude helps shift our focus from lack to abundance, nurturing feelings of joy, contentment, and appreciation. When we practice gratitude, we honor the gifts of life and open ourselves to more blessings.

◆ What to reflect on:

What are you grateful for in your life right now?

How can you express gratitude every day?

What is one thing you've been taking for granted that deserves appreciation?

8. Self-Love

The heart wants you to love yourself fully, to accept yourself with all your flaws and imperfections. It desires you to be kind, patient, and compassionate with yourself. When you love yourself, you can love others in a more authentic and meaningful way. Self-love is the foundation for everything—the more love you give yourself, the more love you can offer the world.

◆ What to reflect on:

How do you show yourself love daily?

Are there areas where you struggle to love yourself?

What can you do today to practice more self-love?

9. Freedom

The heart seeks freedom in all forms—freedom from limiting beliefs, fears, expectations, and constraints. It wants the liberty to express itself without inhibition, to be free of judgment, and to follow its true path. Freedom allows the heart to expand, explore, and create a life that aligns with its deepest desires.

◆ What to reflect on:

Are there areas of your life where you feel restricted or confined?

What does freedom mean to you?

How can you create more freedom in your life today?

10. Joy

Joy is a natural state of the heart. It's the feeling of lightness, of being fully alive in the present moment. When we honor the things that bring us joy, we honor our heart's deepest needs. The heart thrives on experiences that bring happiness and fulfillment—whether it's time spent with loved ones, engaging in hobbies, or simply enjoying life.

◆ What to reflect on:

What activities or people bring you joy?

How often do you make space for joy in your life?

What would your life look like if you prioritized joy every day?

11. Forgiveness

The heart knows that holding onto grudges only weighs it down. Forgiveness is essential for healing and freedom. When we forgive ourselves and others, we release the burden of resentment, creating space for love and peace. Forgiveness doesn't mean forgetting—it means choosing to let go of the emotional charge attached to the pain.

◆ What to reflect on:

Is there someone you need to forgive, including yourself?

How can forgiveness set you free?

What steps can you take to forgive and release the past?

Warmth, compassion, empathy, and bonding are powerful manifestations of what matters deeply to the heart. These qualities allow us to connect more authentically with ourselves and others, fostering deeper relationships, understanding, and healing. Let's explore how these values are intrinsic to the heart's intelligence and why they matter so much.

12. Warmth

The heart craves warmth—not just physical warmth, but emotional warmth that provides a sense of safety and acceptance. When you show warmth to yourself and others, you create a nurturing space where love and trust can thrive. Warmth is the energy that helps you open up, relax, and be vulnerable, knowing that you are embraced for who you are.

◆ What to reflect on:

How do you show warmth to yourself?

Are you open to offering warmth to others, even when it's uncomfortable?

In what ways can you create a warm environment, both within and around you?

13. Compassion

Compassion is one of the deepest expressions of love. It's the ability to truly empathize with another's pain, without judgment, and offer kindness in the face of suffering. The heart desires compassion because it allows healing to take place— both for you and for others. Compassionate acts remind you that we are all connected, and each person's pain is part of the shared human experience.

◆ What to reflect on:

How do you express compassion towards others?

Do you offer the same compassion to yourself during difficult moments?

How can you show more compassion in your daily interactions?

14. Empathy

Empathy is the heart's ability to understand and share the feelings of another. It's about walking in someone else's shoes, feeling their emotions, and offering a safe space to express them. Empathy builds trust and deepens connections. When you listen with empathy, you honor the other person's truth and validate their experiences, which is incredibly healing for both of you.

◆ What to reflect on:

How deeply do you listen when someone is sharing their feelings with you?

Have you ever felt truly understood by someone? How did that impact you?

What would it look like if you practiced more empathy in your relationships?

15. Bonding

At the core of the heart's desires is a deep need for bonding. Bonding with others, whether through friendships, family, or romantic relationships, is vital for emotional well-being. The heart thrives when it connects with another at a soul level. Bonding creates a sense of belonging and safety, and it fosters a shared experience that enriches both individuals.

◆ What to reflect on:

Who do you feel truly bonded with in your life?

Are you investing enough time in nurturing those connections?

What can you do today to strengthen your bonds with others?

16. Heart is Connected to Honoring Soul's Contracts

The heart is the gateway to understanding and fulfilling our soul's purpose. It whispers the wisdom of our soul contracts, guiding us toward the lessons and growth we are meant to experience. When we listen to our heart, we align with the divine path chosen before birth.

Every challenge and joy we encounter is an opportunity to honor these sacred agreements. The heart's deep connection to the soul helps us navigate life with authenticity and purpose. By trusting its guidance, we embrace transformation and move closer to our highest potential. Ignoring the heart's whispers may lead to resistance, but tuning in allows us to walk our destined path with grace.

◆ What to Reflect On:

• How often do you listen to your heart when making important life decisions?

• In what ways has your heart guided you toward fulfilling your soul's purpose?

• How can you strengthen your connection with your heart to better honor your soul contracts?

17. Heart is the Bridge to Reach Your Mind and Body's Desires

The heart serves as the powerful bridge between the mind and body, harmonizing thoughts, emotions, and physical well-being. It translates the mind's desires into feelings and inspires the body to take action. When we listen to our heart, we align our inner wisdom with our external goals, creating a life of balance.

The heart processes emotions in a way the mind cannot, allowing us to make decisions that feel right, not just logical. By tuning into our hearts, we gain clarity on what truly fulfills us on all levels—mental, emotional, and physical. A disconnected heart leads to internal conflict, but when we embrace its wisdom, we achieve harmony and fulfillment.

◆ What to Reflect On:

• How does your heart guide your mind and body toward what truly fulfills you?

• Are there moments when your mind desires something, but your heart feels differently? How do you handle this?

• What practices help you connect with your heart to align your thoughts, emotions, and actions?

What is Heart's Intelligence?

The intelligence of the heart goes beyond logic and reasoning. It is deeply connected to intuition, emotions, and inner wisdom. Here are some key aspects of heart intelligence:

Trusting Yourself – Listening to your intuition and inner guidance.

Emotional Awareness – Recognizing, understanding, and processing emotions effectively.

Compassion – Feeling and expressing genuine care for yourself and others.

Authenticity – Living in alignment with your true self, values, and beliefs.

Resilience – Bouncing back from challenges with grace and inner strength.

Gratitude – Acknowledging and appreciating life's blessings, both big and small.

Forgiveness – Letting go of resentment and embracing healing and peace.

Presence – Being fully in the moment, connected to yourself and the world around you.

Courage – Following your heart even when it requires stepping into the unknown.

Love & Connection – Creating deep, meaningful relationships based on trust and empathy.

Alignment with Purpose and Values - Helps you connect to your true purpose and live in alignment with your core values.

Healing Power - Holds the ability to heal emotional wounds and physical imbalances. When we access the wisdom of the heart, we can tap into deeper healing, not just for our emotions, but also for our bodies

Intuitive Knowing - Knows things before the mind can comprehend them, the feeling of a "gut instinct" or a knowing that guides us in the right direction.

The Connection Between Mind and Heart – It is the bridge between the mind and body, where the mind seeks understanding through logic, and the heart provides understanding through feeling

The Connection Between Mind and Body– Acts as a bridge between the mind and body, creating harmony by aligning thoughts, emotions, and physical well-being.

The Connection Between Mind and Soul – Serves as a bridge between the mind and soul, helping us access deeper wisdom and align our thoughts with our higher purpose.

Damages you do when you don't listen to your heart's intelligence

When you ignore or suppress the intelligence of your heart, the consequences can be profound, affecting not only your emotional well-being but also your physical health, relationships, and overall life satisfaction. Your heart, being the center of your emotional awareness, intuition, and connection, offers wisdom that helps you live authentically and harmoniously. Ignoring this wisdom can lead to numerous forms of damage, both internal and external. Let's explore the potential consequences of not listening to the heart's intelligence:

1. Emotional Drainage

When you neglect your heart's wisdom, you may push down emotions or avoid dealing with them, thinking that they'll go away on their own. But emotions, especially unprocessed ones, don't disappear. They build up and create emotional turbulence. This can lead to chronic stress, anxiety, sadness, or even feelings of emptiness. Ignoring your heart's cues can eventually manifest in emotional burnout, leaving you feeling emotionally drained and disconnected.

Impact:

Increased stress levels

Persistent feelings of sadness or numbness

A disconnect from your true feelings, causing confusion and frustration

2. Lack of Authenticity

Your heart knows who you are—your essence, your true self. But when you disregard its intelligence, you may end up wearing a mask to please others, fitting into societal norms, or adhering to expectations that aren't in alignment with your soul. This creates a deep sense of inauthenticity and inner conflict.

Impact:

Living a life that feels untrue to who you are

Constantly seeking external validation

A lack of self-fulfillment, which leads to dissatisfaction and confusion about your purpose

3. Physical Health Decline

The body and mind are intricately connected. When you ignore the emotional signals from your heart, your body may start to show signs of distress. Chronic suppression of emotions, especially stress or unexpressed grief, has been linked to various physical ailments such as tension headaches, digestive issues, high blood pressure, and weakened immune function.

Impact:

Increased risk of physical ailments due to emotional suppression

Weakened immune system, leaving you more vulnerable to illness

Chronic pain or tension, especially in areas like the shoulders, neck, or lower back

4. Weakened Relationships

At the core of any relationship—whether with yourself, a partner, family, or friends— is the ability to connect deeply. When you ignore your heart's wisdom, it becomes difficult to truly listen to others or express yourself authentically. This often results in misunderstandings, communication breakdowns, and a sense of emotional disconnection.

Impact:

Difficulty forming deep, meaningful connections with others

Miscommunication and unresolved conflict

Growing resentment or feelings of isolation

5. Unfulfilled Dreams and Desires

Your heart holds the blueprint of your deepest desires, aspirations, and purpose in life. Ignoring its intelligence can lead to neglecting your dreams and passions. Whether due to fear, societal pressure, or self-doubt, not listening to the heart can cause you to miss out on opportunities that would bring you joy, fulfillment, and purpose.

Impact:

Feeling stuck or uninspired in your career or personal life

A growing sense of regret or "what could have been"

Missed opportunities that could have led to growth or fulfillment

6. Increased Fear and Anxiety

The heart is often a source of guidance in times of uncertainty. It helps you tap into your intuition and sense of trust. When you ignore it, you may find yourself overthinking or making decisions out of fear rather than wisdom. This causes an imbalance, heightening anxiety and fear.

Impact:

Increased stress and anxiety about the future

Fear-driven decisions that don't align with your true desires

Difficulty trusting your instincts or making confident choices

7. Self-Sabotage

When you don't listen to your heart, you may act in ways that are counterproductive to your well-being and growth. This can manifest as procrastination, self-doubt, perfectionism, or avoiding challenges that would help you grow. The result? You remain stuck in a cycle of self-sabotage.

Impact:

Repeated patterns of procrastination or avoidance

Lack of progress toward goals, leaving you feeling stagnant

Self-criticism and diminished self-worth

8. Loss of Connection to Purpose

Your heart's intelligence is directly connected to your life's purpose. It helps you understand what truly matters to you and guides you toward meaningful work, relationships, and experiences. Ignoring your heart's wisdom can lead to a loss of connection to your greater purpose, causing feelings of aimlessness or confusion.

Impact:

A sense of emptiness or lack of direction

Feeling disconnected from your life's deeper meaning

Struggling to find motivation or passion in daily activities

9. Emotional Repression

Repressing your emotions, especially out of fear of judgment or rejection, can lead to emotional volatility and unhealthy coping mechanisms. When your heart's messages are ignored, emotions like sadness, anger, or joy may be suppressed until they explode or manifest in negative ways.

Impact:

Emotional outbursts or mood swings

Internalized anger or frustration

Difficulty managing emotions in a healthy way

10. Spiritual Disconnect

The heart is often considered the gateway to your spiritual connection. When you ignore its intelligence, you may experience a sense of spiritual disconnection or feel distant from your higher self. This can lead to feelings of loneliness, confusion, or even a lack of meaning in life.

Impact:

A sense of isolation or loneliness

Disconnection from your inner truth or spiritual beliefs

Feeling disconnected from the divine or your spiritual essence

Conclusion:

The Importance of Listening to Your Heart

The heart's intelligence is a vital source of guidance, strength, and healing. By tuning into its wisdom, we not only avoid the damage of ignoring it but also open ourselves to greater joy, fulfillment, and peace. When you listen to your heart, you reconnect with your true self, experience deeper connections with others, and walk a path of authenticity and purpose. Ignoring it, on the other hand, leads to a life of Stagnation, confusion, and disconnection.

Not to forget, the soul enters the mother's womb with a divine purpose, carrying sacred contracts meant for growth. It whispers its guidance through the heart, nudging us toward the path we are meant to walk. When we truly listen to the heart's wisdom, we align with the soul's higher plan. Each experience, whether joyful or painful, is an opportunity to honor these soul agreements. By trusting our heart's whispers, we navigate life with clarity, authenticity, and purpose. And when our journey is complete, the soul gracefully departs, continuing its eternal evolution.

So, how can you begin to honor your heart's wisdom today? What steps can you take to listen more deeply to what your heart is saying? Let's dive deep into it.

The 9 Untold Truths

1. The Heart Speaks in Silence

2. Pain Unlocks Its Secrets

3. The Heart Holds Emotional Memory & Influences Your Thoughts and Emotions

4. Your Heart Speaks to Your Body: The Silent Language of Emotions & Health

5. The heart is connected to your intuition and creativity- Your Heart Knows More Than You Think!

6. The Heart's Intelligence Can Heal You – It Holds Infinite Wisdom

7. The Heart is the Seat of Consciousness

8. Heart Guides You Toward Authenticity

9. The Heart Holds the Blueprint of Your Purpose

These nine truths are the key to unlocking the immense power of your heart's intelligence. Each chapter will dive deeper into one of these truths, offering practical tools, insights, and exercises to help you reconnect with your heart and live a more fulfilled, authentic life.

By the end of this book, you will have discovered the profound wisdom within your heart and learned how to align with it to live a life of greater purpose, creativity, health, and emotional freedom.

Let's begin this transformative journey— one that will not only change the way you see your heart but also the way you live your life.

Chapter 1

Truth 1: The Heart Speaks in Silence

Have you ever noticed how, in the middle of chaos, your heart sometimes offers you a moment of clarity? That gentle pull, the unshakable knowing, the warmth in your chest when something just *feels* right—it's as if your heart carries a wisdom beyond words. Yet, how often do we truly listen?

In a world that glorifies logic and proof, we're conditioned to rely on the mind— analyzing, calculating, and seeking evidence before making a move. But have you ever made a decision that defied logic, yet turned out to be the best choice? A time when you just *knew* something without being able to explain it? What if the heart holds an intelligence that the mind simply cannot grasp?

Think about it: Your mind processes thoughts, but your heart *feels* truth. Your mind calculates risk, but your heart *senses* alignment. Your mind might tell you a path is safe, but your heart might whisper that it isn't right for you. How often have you ignored those whispers, only to realize later that your heart was right all along?

What if true wisdom isn't just about knowledge but about connection—to yourself, to your intuition, to something greater? What if the heart isn't just an organ but a compass, guiding you through the noise, towards what truly matters?

So, pause for a moment. Breathe. Can you feel it? That quiet, steady presence in your chest, the one that's been with you all along? What is it telling you right now? And are you ready to listen?

The Silent Voice of the Heart

The heart has its language, doesn't it? It doesn't speak in words or logic, yet somehow, it *knows*. Have you ever felt that quiet certainty deep inside you—like an unshakable truth—before your mind even had a chance to catch up? That's the heart speaking.

It's subtle, almost like a whisper. It doesn't push or demand, and it certainly doesn't argue the way the mind does. Instead, it speaks through sensations—a lightness in your chest when something feels right, a quiet peace in the middle of uncertainty, or even a tight knot when something isn't meant for you. Have you ever ignored that feeling, only to realize later that your heart was right all along?

But here's the challenge: The world is loud. Our minds are even louder. Have you noticed how quickly we fill every moment with noise—work, meetings, the endless stream of social media, the ping of a new message, and the constant buzz of notifications? We're constantly absorbing information, analyzing situations, and weighing pros and cons. We're in a perpetual race, running from one task to the next, always feeling like we need to do more, be more, have more.

It's easy to forget that the heart speaks in the quiet spaces. It's easy to lose touch with those whispers when we're constantly bombarded by the noise of our daily lives. How often do you find yourself scrolling mindlessly through your phone, distracted by the endless scroll, the next post, the next video? Have you ever stopped to wonder: How much of your time are you truly giving to the most important thing—yourself?

When was the last time you *paused*? Not just a quick break to check your email or reply to a message, but a genuine pause—just to breathe, just to *be*? How often do we allow ourselves the gift of silence, especially when we live in a world that's constantly pulling us in different directions? How much time do we truly give to *listening* to our own heart?

We've become so accustomed to distractions that silence feels uncomfortable at times. We rush through the day, trying to keep up with the never-ending to-do lists, and before we know it, hours or even days have passed without us giving any real attention to our inner wisdom. What if the heart's whispers are drowned out by all this noise, simply because we haven't created the space to hear them?

So, I ask you: How often do you create time in your busy schedule for silence? How much time do you dedicate to just sitting with your breath, with your thoughts, with the stillness that allows your heart to speak? What would change if you made it a point to pause, even for just a few moments throughout the day, to listen to the whispers and feel the peace that lies within the quiet spaces?

Amid the chaos, the race to get ahead, and the distractions that pull us in all directions, are we willing to permit ourselves to slow down? To listen? To hear the silent guidance of our hearts?

Take a moment right now—what if you *gave* yourself that time? What if, just for a minute, you let go of everything else and tuned in? What might your heart be telling you?

Think back to a time when you felt an unexplained sense of peace, even when things weren't logically "perfect." Or a time when everything seemed fine on the surface, but deep down, something felt *off*.

Did you trust that feeling? Or did you let your mind talk you out of it?

What if the heart's wisdom isn't something to be understood, but something to be felt? What if, instead of always searching for logical reasons, we simply allowed ourselves to trust the way our heart responds? That intuitive nudge, that deep sense of knowing that doesn't need a list of facts to justify its existence—it just *feels right*.

To all the left-brain ruled people, logical people, highly intellectual, the CEOs, the strategists, the thinkers, and decision-makers out there—this one's for you. I know your minds are powerful, sharp, and always calculating the best path forward. But here's the truth: even the sharpest mind can miss the mark if it forgets the heart.

When was the last time you trusted your gut, your intuition, that inner feeling that tells you when something is aligned or when it's off—without needing to prove it with numbers or logic? How many times have you made decisions based on strategy and intellect alone, only to realize later that your heart was telling you something different all along?

In the world of high stakes, constant demands, and tight deadlines, it's easy to dismiss feelings as "soft" or "irrational." But I urge you to consider: could your feelings be the key to something even more powerful? Could the wisdom of the heart—when embraced—bring clarity that logic alone cannot provide?

The heart doesn't always need evidence or data. It simply knows. And sometimes, that knowing is exactly what we need to make decisions that are truly aligned with our deepest values and purpose.

So, I ask you: What if, in your pursuit of excellence, you also listened to your heart? What if, in those critical moments of decision-making, you allowed yourself to pause and check in with your feelings? Could you create a more holistic, harmonious path forward—not just with your intellect, but with the deep wisdom of your heart?

Take a moment. Close your eyes. Breathe. What is your heart telling you right now? And are you ready to listen? Hmm, I know your mind is telling you something, is there a battle?

The Battle Between the Heart and the Mind

Let's face it, we're wired to listen to our minds, right? We're trained to think, analyze, plan, strategize, find reasons, and solve problems. The mind is a great tool, but it can also be a noisy one. It's constantly talking, constantly planning, constantly judging. And sometimes, in the middle of all that noise, it's easy to forget about the gentle whispers from the heart.

What if I told you that the mind and heart often have two completely different agendas? The mind wants to control, rationalize, to plan for the future. The heart, on the other hand, speaks to us in a language of feeling, intuition, and truth. It doesn't care about your to-do list; it just knows what's best for your soul.

Can you think of a time when your mind was telling you one thing, but your heart was pulling you in a completely different direction? What happened when you chose to listen to the mind, rather than the heart? And how did that turn out for you?

The heart's message is softer, quieter, and often more subtle than the mind's loud demands. But it's in those soft moments of stillness and silence that we hear the heart's deepest truths. And when we ignore it, well, let's just say life has a funny way of reminding us what happens when we don't listen to what's truly important.

Would you like to know how to lessen the noise between mind and heart? Learn to listen to the silence between the inhale and exhale.

Silence: The Secret to Hearing Your Heart

So, how do we tap into the heart's wisdom? It's simple: we slow down. We create space for silence. In a world that's constantly asking us to do more, be more, have more— it's essential to pause. To take a deep breath. To simply be.

Have you ever noticed that space—the one between your inhales and exhales? It's subtle, almost invisible, yet it's there, holding everything together. That space, that quiet moment, is where true stillness lives. The breath comes in, and the breath goes out—but it's the silence between them that holds the key to everything. Isn't it curious how in that brief moment of pause, we can hear ourselves the clearest?

When was the last time you truly paid attention to that space between breaths? How often do we rush through our day, inhaling and exhaling, without ever noticing the beauty in the stillness between them? What if, just for a moment, you allowed yourself to feel that silence? To let go of the constant rush and instead, simply breathe?

Think about it: your breath is designed for balance. Inhaling brings in life, vitality, and new energy. Exhaling lets go of what no longer serves you. So, why not extend this to your emotions? Why not breathe in positivity, love, and clarity, and exhale the negativity, stress, and tension that weigh you down? Imagine how much lighter you'd feel, how much more open to receiving the wisdom your heart has been whispering all along.

Have you ever sat quietly for just a few minutes, without any distractions, without reaching for your phone, or worrying about the next thing on your to-do list? It might feel strange at first, maybe even uncomfortable, but that's okay. The more you practice sitting in this silence, the more you'll begin to hear your heart speak. The more you'll begin to feel its gentle guidance in your body, in your breath, in the stillness.

So, what if the key to hearing your heart's wisdom isn't about thinking harder or searching outside of yourself, but about simply creating space for silence? What if, in the pause, you find everything you've been looking for? Take a moment now, breathe deeply, and notice the silence. What is it telling you?

Are you ready to create that space for yourself?

Remember, The Heart Speaks in Silence

The heart doesn't shout; it whispers. Its wisdom comes through intuition, gut feelings, and a deep sense of knowing. Often, when we quiet our minds through meditation or mindfulness, we can hear its subtle guidance. It's in those moments of stillness that the heart's voice becomes the loudest.

Have you ever felt an unexplainable pull towards something—a choice, a person, or even a moment? That's your heart speaking, not in words, but in whispers that only you can understand. Let me share two relatable examples to help you tune into this silent language.

The Unexplainable Calm

Imagine this: You're stuck in a dilemma about a big decision—maybe a job offer, a relationship, or a move. Logically, everything seems perfect on paper, but something inside you hesitates. Then one day, during a quiet walk or as you stare at the stars, a wave of calm washes over you. It's as if your heart whispers, *"This is what you truly want."*

Have you ever felt this calm clarity? What would happen if you paused today to listen to what your heart might be trying to say?

The Restlessness That Won't Go Away

Sometimes, the heart doesn't whisper gently—it nudges persistently. You might feel restless in a situation—a career that drains you, a relationship that feels heavy, or a path that no longer excites you. No matter how much you try to ignore it, the unease lingers. That's your heart saying, *"This isn't where you're meant to be."* What if you took a moment right now to sit with that restlessness and ask yourself, "What is my heart guiding me towards? What am I afraid to acknowledge?"

Your heart speaks, not in words, but in feelings, nudges, and silent knowing. Can you hear it? What might change in your life if you trusted its whispers today?

Have you ever noticed how the most profound truths don't come in a burst of noise but in the quietest moments? The heart doesn't demand attention; it whispers. Its wisdom doesn't arrive with fanfare; it seeps into your being like a gentle breeze. But how often do we slow down enough to listen?

In a world that glorifies busyness and noise, the heart's voice often gets drowned out. Its messages come through intuition—a gut feeling, a subtle pull, or a sense of knowing that words can't quite describe. Have you ever had a moment when you just knew something, even though you couldn't explain why? That's your heart speaking, softly but unmistakably.

Can you recall the last time you truly sat in stillness? Not to plan, analyze, or solve, but simply to be? That's where the heart's voice becomes the loudest—in the stillness, in the pauses, in the silence between your thoughts.

Think about it: When you feel lost or overwhelmed, your first instinct might be to search for answers outside yourself. But what if the answers are already within? What if the clarity you seek is waiting for you to quiet the noise and tune in to the wisdom of your own heart?

Here's the truth: the heart doesn't compete for your attention. It won't shout over the chaos of your mind or the chatter of the world. It waits—patiently, lovingly—for you to create space for it. It will give you one nudge and then silence the voice. The heart's whispers aren't always logical, but they're always truthful. It might guide you toward a choice that seems unconventional or nudge you to walk away from something that no longer serves you. Have you ever ignored a gut feeling, only to realize later it was right all along? That's the heart's gentle way of reminding you: I'm here. I've always been here. You just need to listen.

Ask yourself: What is my heart trying to tell me right now that my mind might be ignoring?

When was the last time I trusted my intuition, and how did it lead me?

How can I create more moments of silence in my day to truly hear my inner voice?

The heart speaks in a language beyond words—a language of emotions, sensations, and a deep sense of connection to your true self. When you learn to listen, you unlock a wellspring of wisdom that's been waiting for you all along.

So, take a moment today. Sit in silence. Breathe deeply.

Place your hand on your heart and ask, what do you want me to know?

You might be surprised by what you hear. Because in the quiet, your heart has a way of saying exactly what you need—softly, gently, and with infinite love. For that, you need to trust yourself.

How to listen to the heart's whispers? By trusting yourself

Trusting Yourself

Have you ever had a gut feeling about something, but you ignored it, only to realize later that your intuition was right all along? That is your heart speaking to you. It is the part of you that *knows*, even when logic cannot explain why.

Trusting yourself means honoring your inner voice, even when it contradicts external opinions. Too often, we seek validation from others—family, friends, colleagues—before making decisions. We doubt our wisdom, fearing that we might make the "wrong" choice. But have you ever considered that not deciding for yourself *is* a real mistake?

The heart's intelligence is subtle yet powerful. It speaks in gentle nudges, inner whispers, and deep emotions. It tells you when something feels right, and when it doesn't. But are you listening? Or are you drowning it out with self-doubt, overthinking, and external noise?

Think about it—how many times have you second-guessed yourself, only to realize later that you had the answer all along? What stopped you from trusting yourself in the first place? Was it fear? Was it a past failure? Or was it the habit of looking outside for answers rather than within?

Your heart carries the wisdom of your entire life's experiences, your deepest truths, and your soul's calling. But trust is a muscle—it strengthens with practice. The more you trust yourself, the more confident and aligned you become.

Questions for Reflection:

◆ *What is one decision you made that you later regretted because you didn't trust yourself?*
◆ *How would your life be different if you always trusted your inner wisdom?*
◆ *What stops you from listening to your heart?*

Actionable Steps to Strengthen Self-Trust:

Pause and Listen – Every day, take 5 minutes to check in with yourself. Place your hand on your heart and ask, *"What do I truly feel?"* Write down whatever comes up.

Act on Small Instincts – If your heart nudges you to do something—call a friend, say no to something that doesn't feel right, take a leap—*do it*. Start with small decisions and watch your confidence grow.

Silence the Inner Critic – Notice when self-doubt creeps in. Instead of engaging with it, ask yourself, *"What if I trusted myself instead?"*

Reflect on Past Wins – Think of a time when trusting yourself led to something great. Write it down as a reminder that your intuition is powerful.

Affirmations for Trust – Repeat: *"I trust myself. My heart knows the way. My inner wisdom is my greatest guide."*

The truth is, you already have all the answers you seek. The question is—will you trust yourself enough to follow them?

What makes you feel light, is always right for you. – Roop Lakhani

Yes, let the heart feel light always. Have you ever had that inner voice telling you that something feels right or something doesn't, even when your mind can't explain why? Listening to the whispers of your heart is one of the most powerful ways to connect with your true self. But here's the thing: the heart doesn't shout. It speaks gently, often through feelings, sensations, and a quiet knowing that rises within you. How often do we rush through life, distracted by external noise, without pausing to hear what our heart is trying to tell us?

Have you ever had that inner voice that tells you *this is the right path* or *this doesn't feel right* even when your mind can't explain why? That's your heart guiding you.

So, how do we start tuning into this beautiful, subtle guidance? Let's explore together.

How to tune to the whispers of what the heart is saying?

1. Creating Space for Silence

Isn't it funny how the busier we get, the harder it becomes to hear our inner voice? In the hustle of everyday life, we can forget to listen to what's happening inside us. What if you set aside just a few moments of silence each day?

Have you ever tried sitting in stillness for a few minutes and just listening to what comes up? What does your heart whisper when you allow yourself to just be? The more you practice creating space for silence, the easier it becomes to hear the heart's voice.

2. Feeling Into Your Body

Our bodies are incredible at sending us signals—tightness in the chest, warmth around the heart, fluttering sensations—these are all messages from the heart. Have you ever felt your heart race when something excites you? Or that calm peace when you make a decision that feels aligned with your soul?

What do you notice in your body when you think about a decision or situation? Can you feel a sense of expansion or contraction? When was the last time you tuned into your body and let it guide you?

3. Trusting Your Gut

Sometimes, your heart speaks in that little gut feeling. That feeling you get when you *just know* something is right, even if logic doesn't back it up.

Have you ever had a moment where you followed your gut and it turned out to be exactly what you needed? Maybe it was a choice that didn't make sense at the time, but you felt a deep knowing. What if that's your heart speaking to you? Are you willing to trust those moments, even when the reasoning doesn't add up?

4. Checking In with Your Heart's Desires

How often do you take the time to ask yourself, *what does my heart truly want right now?* We can get so caught up in life's demands and expectations, but your heart knows what brings you joy, peace, and fulfillment.

Do you take the time to listen to that inner desire? What does your heart long for, deep down? It might be as simple as more rest, a change in routine, or the courage to take that leap of faith. Are you allowing yourself to ask and listen?

5. Recognizing Patterns and Repeated Nudges

Have you noticed certain themes or patterns that keep showing up in your life? Maybe it's a feeling or a situation that repeats itself. Do you ever wonder if your heart is trying to tell you something?

When you reflect on these repeated nudges, what do you feel? What's your heart trying to guide you toward, and are you open to seeing it?

6. Practicing Heart-Centered Practices

Heart-centered practices, like meditation, journaling, or even a simple breath-focused moment, can be powerful ways to create a deeper connection to your heart.
What practices have you tried that help you connect with your heart? How do they make you feel afterward? Imagine making these practices a part of your daily life— how might they transform your connection to your heart's whispers?

7. Letting Go of Fear and Judgment

Fear and judgment can be major blocks when it comes to listening to your heart. The heart speaks in quiet, soft tones, and fear can drown it out with loud, critical thoughts.
What fears or doubts arise when you think about trusting your heart? What if you could let go of the need to be perfect or to have all the answers? How much more peace and clarity might you experience if

you allowed yourself to simply trust your heart's wisdom?

8. Reflecting on Past Experiences

Think about the times in your life when you *did* listen to your heart. Maybe it wasn't the easiest choice, but it felt like the right one. What happened afterward? How did it feel to follow your heart's guidance?
Can you recall a moment when you trusted your heart, even though others around you might have doubted you? What did that decision teach you about yourself and your heart's wisdom?

Your heart is always speaking to you, guiding you toward your highest good. Are you ready to listen? The more you practice, the clearer those whispers will become, and soon, you'll be able to trust your heart without hesitation. Your heart has the wisdom and love that you need to navigate life—are you willing to honor it?

Tuning Into the Heart: Listening to the Heart's Whispers

We have spent so much of our lives listening to the loud, demanding voices of our minds. The mind wants answers, solutions, and logic—it's a master of strategy and planning. But the heart? The heart speaks in whispers, and to hear it, we must slow down and tune in. So, how can we start to listen to the heart's subtle nudges? Here are a few practices to help you tune into the heart's wisdom.

1. Mindfulness: The Art of Presence

Mindfulness is all about being present—truly present—in the moment. When you are fully engaged in the present, free from distractions, your heart's messages become clearer. The key is to notice how you feel, without judgment. Mindfulness helps you separate the heart's quiet signals from the louder, often more chaotic thoughts of the mind.

Here's a simple mindfulness exercise to begin with:

Mindful Breathing Exercise:

Find a quiet space where you can sit comfortably.

Close your eyes and bring your attention to your breath.

Take a slow, deep breath in, and then exhale.

With each breath, allow yourself to focus solely on the sensation of breathing. Feel the rise and fall of your chest or belly.

As you breathe, start to notice what's going on inside. Are there any subtle feelings in your chest area? What emotions are present?

Simply observe them without labeling or trying to change them. Allow these feelings to pass through you, like clouds floating by.

Breathing deeply not only relaxes the body but also creates a sense of space for the heart's wisdom to emerge. Now do deep breathing. Deep breathing helps to shift your focus from your busy thoughts to your body—and when you connect to your body, you connect to your heart.

Deep Breathing Exercise:

Sit comfortably and place one hand on your heart.

Inhale deeply through your nose, counting to four.

Hold your breath for a moment, then exhale slowly for a count of four.

With each exhale, imagine releasing any tension or mental chatter, and allowing your heart space to breathe.

As you continue breathing deeply, ask yourself: "What does my heart want me to know today?"

Don't force an answer, just let whatever comes naturally arise—whether it's a feeling, a thought, or a sense of clarity.

This simple practice can help you clear the noise of the mind and make room for the stillness where your heart speaks.

2. Quiet Reflection: Asking Your Heart for Guidance

When we're constantly rushing, it's easy to forget to reflect and listen to our inner wisdom. Reflection allows us to process our feelings, think things through, and make sense of the emotions that arise. By setting aside time each day to reflect quietly, you create an opportunity for your heart to be heard.

Here's a guided reflection exercise to help you tap into your heart's wisdom:

Heart Reflection Exercise:

Take 10-15 minutes at the start or end of your day to sit quietly.

Close your eyes, and with your hands resting gently on your lap, focus on your heart area.

Take a few deep breaths and ask yourself:

"What does my heart need me to know today?"

"Where am I being called to align with my true self?"

"How can I honor my heart in this moment?"

Let the answers come naturally—don't try to force or rationalize them. Just sit in the silence and feel what arises. You might feel a shift in your body, a sudden insight, or a gentle nudge.

After this, take a moment to write down what you felt or thought. Often, the heart speaks more clearly when we put our feelings into words.

3. Body Scan: Listening Through Sensations

Our body is deeply connected to the heart's intelligence, and it often speaks through physical sensations. Have you ever noticed a tight feeling in your chest or a sense of lightness in your body when something feels right? These sensations are the body's way of communicating what the heart feels.

Here's a Body Scan to help you tune into the heart's messages through physical sensations:

Body Scan Exercise:

Find a quiet, comfortable space to sit or lie down.

Close your eyes, take a deep breath, and begin by scanning your body from head to toe.

Start at the top of your head and slowly move your attention down to your toes.

As you focus on each area of your body, ask yourself: "How does this part of my body feel right now?"

Notice any sensations—tension, warmth, tightness, lightness, or relaxation.

When you reach your chest or heart area, ask: "What is my heart telling me through this sensation?"

Simply observe and allow yourself to feel the messages without judgment.

Your body is a treasure chest of wisdom, and tuning into it can help you hear the heart's whispers more clearly.

4. Journaling: Documenting the Heart's Wisdom

Sometimes the heart speaks in ways we don't immediately understand. Journaling is a great tool to help translate those whispers into clarity. Writing down your thoughts, feelings, and intuitions can bring out profound insights from your heart.

Try this exercise to open up a deeper conversation with your heart through journaling:

Heart-Centered Journaling Exercise:

Set aside a quiet moment to sit with your journal.

Ask yourself: "What is my heart trying to tell me today?"

Write freely and let the words flow without filtering them.

Don't worry about grammar or structure — just focus on expressing what's in your heart.

After you've written for a few minutes, reflect on what came up. Were there any surprising insights or feelings that emerged?

This exercise allows you to capture the heart's voice and make sense of it over time.

It helps you create a deeper connection with your inner truth.

Wrap-Up: Trusting Your Heart's Whispers

Listening to the heart's wisdom takes practice, patience, and an open mind. But once you start tuning in—whether through mindfulness, deep breathing, quiet reflection, body scan, or journalling—you'll find that the heart has so much to share with you.

You may start to notice that you feel more aligned, more at peace, and more connected to your true self. And when you honor your heart's wisdom, the world around you starts to make more sense, and your path becomes clearer.

So, what does your heart want you to know today? Are you ready to listen?

Which ones have you started?

Not yet!

Still reading further!

Reminder, pause and take the time out!

Chapter 2

Truth 2: Pain Unlocks Its Secrets

Pain. We all encounter it at some point in our lives—whether it's emotional, physical, or even spiritual. But what if I told you that pain, as much as it hurts, could be a gateway to a deeper understanding of yourself? What if the pain you've been avoiding or struggling with could unlock hidden wisdom within your heart, leading you toward healing, growth, and self-awareness?

The greatest lessons of the heart often emerge through pain. Heartbreak, loss, and challenges force us to dig deep, reevaluate our priorities, and grow stronger. Pain cracks open the heart, allowing its wisdom to flow freely. It's through these cracks that we learn resilience, compassion, and self-love.

Have you ever wondered why pain feels so unbearable yet so transformative? Why, amid heartbreak or loss, life feels shattered, but later, those cracks seem to glow with a light you didn't know was there? What if pain isn't a punishment, but a teacher—one that holds the keys to your deepest growth and truest wisdom?

Pain has a way of breaking us open. It forces us to stop, to sit in the rawness of our emotions, and to ask the questions we've been avoiding: What truly matters to me? What am I holding onto that no longer serves me? Who am I beyond this moment of suffering?

When the heart breaks—whether through loss, betrayal, failure or even regret—it doesn't just fall apart. It opens. And in that opening, it reveals the parts of you that are hidden beneath the surface: your resilience, your compassion, your courage to move forward. Isn't it strange how the most painful experiences often teach us the most about love, forgiveness, and strength?

Take a moment to think back to a time when pain felt unbearable. What did it teach you? Did it reveal a strength you didn't know you had? Did it force you to let go of something you were clinging to too tightly?

Or perhaps, did it remind you of the importance of self-love, self-worth, or setting boundaries?

Pain is the heart's way of saying; something needs to change. It strips away the masks, the pretenses, and the distractions, leaving you face-to-face with your truth. Yes, it hurts. But it also awakens. It's through those cracks that wisdom begins to flow— the kind of wisdom that no book, no advice, and no external force could ever teach you.

There's beauty in those cracks, isn't there? The scars of your heart are not signs of weakness; they are proof of survival, growth, and transformation.

Ask yourself:

What has my pain taught me about who I am?

How has heartbreak or loss shaped my understanding of love and connection?

What would I not have discovered about myself had I not faced this challenge?

Pain, as unbearable as it feels in the moment, is often the catalyst for the most profound self-discovery. It teaches you to let go, to forgive, to heal, and most importantly, to love yourself through it all. When the storm passes, you emerge stronger, wiser, and more compassionate— not despite the pain, but because of it. So, the next time pain knocks at your door, remember: it's not here to break you; it's here to transform you. Let it guide you to the secrets your heart has been waiting to reveal.

It's remarkable how many artists, singers, poets, and authors have channeled their deepest pain into their creative works, unveiling their true potential. It's almost as if the pain they experience becomes the canvas for their creativity, allowing them to channel emotions into something universally relatable. Pain, as difficult as it is, often becomes a catalyst for transformation. It forces us to look within, confront the darkness, and emerge with something profound, something that resonates not only with us but with others too.

For example, when we listen to a singer like Arijit Singh or read the verses of poets like Rumi or Deepak Chopra, we often feel as though they are speaking directly to us because their art is born from their personal suffering, vulnerabilities, and healing. Their wounds become the wellspring from which their art emerges, allowing them to communicate raw, unfiltered emotions that touch the hearts of their audience.

Similarly, as healers, we often experience pain ourselves—not as something to remain stuck in, but as a catalyst for growth and healing. Just like me, many healers face their challenges and struggles. But it's through working through those pains that we gain insights, wisdom, and tools to help others on their journey. Our healed stories become the foundation for our work, enabling us to empathize deeply with the people we help and guide them toward their healing.

The pain is not an end—it's a starting point. It's the crucible in which we are refined, and from it, both art and healing emerge. When we allow ourselves to heal, we gain not only personal growth but also the ability to help others rise from their wounds. It's through our own healed stories that we can bring light to the dark spaces in others' lives.

The Wisdom Within Pain

It's easy to view pain as something to escape or resist, isn't it? Whether it's the ache of a broken heart, the sharp sting of betrayal, the weight of failure, or even the discomfort of chronic illness, pain often feels like an enemy. We push it away, deny it, or try to distract ourselves from it, hoping it'll go away. But what if, instead of running from pain, we allowed ourselves to embrace it? What if it's trying to tell us something important, something we need to hear?

Think about it for a moment. Have you ever experienced emotional pain that, at the time, felt unbearable—only to later realize that it was a catalyst for positive change in your life? Like falling in love deeply, only to face heartache later. At the time, the pain feels like it will never end, but in hindsight, it often turns out to be the very experience that teaches you more about yourself, about boundaries, and about what truly matters.

Or maybe you've had a moment where you trusted someone blindly—whether it was a friend, a colleague, or a partner—and they broke that trust. The betrayal stung. But what did that pain teach you? It might have opened your eyes to a new level of discernment. It could have shown you that your trust is precious, and now, you know to protect it more carefully.

Maybe you've lent money to a friend, only to have them never return it. That sting of disappointment can feel like betrayal, but what if it's also teaching you a valuable lesson in setting boundaries around your generosity? Or maybe you've shared your secrets, your heart, with someone you thought was trustworthy, only to find that they manipulated you or broke your trust. The pain cuts deep, but it also reveals your strength and teaches you the importance of trusting your instincts and recognizing the people who truly deserve a place in your life.

Have you ever experienced physical pain that later led to a profound shift in your perspective? Maybe an injury or illness forced you to slow down, to pay attention to your body in a way you never had before. You might have realized how much you've been pushing yourself, and how little you've been nurturing your well-being. And as painful as it was, that physical discomfort became the wake-up call you needed to begin making healthier choices.

What if, instead of running from pain, we leaned into it? What if we saw it as an invitation rather than a burden? Pain, in all its forms, can reveal parts of us that need attention, love, and healing. It's through pain that we learn what's truly important to us—what we value, what we're capable of, and what we need to let go of. Sometimes, it's the most painful experiences that teach us the deepest lessons about ourselves and our lives.

So, I ask you: Have you ever thought about what pain is trying to teach you? Rather than resist it, could you be open to receiving the wisdom it holds? What might shift if you allowed yourself to embrace your pain as a teacher, rather than an enemy?

Real life examples

Let's talk about some remarkable people who have used pain as a stepping stone, turning their struggles into strength and inspiration for millions.

Take **Amitabh Bachchan**ji, for example. Here's a man who, at the age of 82, is still working tirelessly in the film industry, defying the odds and proving that age is just a number. Recently, he completed 25 years of hosting the popular game show *Kaun Banega Crorepati*, a testament to his unparalleled work ethic and timeless appeal. His journey from a struggling actor to one of India's most beloved icons shows the power of perseverance and passion. Bachchan's story inspires millions, proving that age is just a number when you have dedication and drive. Not only did he face immense financial challenges when his production company, ABCL, collapsed, but he also went through a period where his career seemed to be on a decline. Yet, he rose from those struggles, not only financially but also in terms of his legacy. His resilience is a testament to the fact that pain doesn't have to define you. Instead, it can fuel your determination to keep going, no matter the obstacles.

And we can't forget **Priyanka Chopra.** From winning the title of Miss World to becoming one of the most successful inspiring motivating actresses globally, Priyanka's journey has been anything but easy. She's spoken about her struggles with bullying, personal loss, and the immense pressure to constantly perform. Yet, Priyanka has turned her pain into motivation, using her platform to inspire others, particularly women. She has built a life of resilience, and in the process, her own experiences with pain have fueled her desire to empower others. She shares her journey openly, encouraging others to rise above challenges with grace and determination.

Helen Keller was born in 1880 and lost both her sight and hearing at 19 months due to an illness. Despite these challenges, she learned to communicate through the help of her dedicated teacher, Anne Sullivan. Keller became the first deaf-blind person to earn a college degree, graduating from Radcliffe College in 1904. She wrote several books and gave countless speeches, advocating for people with disabilities, women's rights, and social causes. Helen became an international symbol of strength, perseverance, and human potential. Her legacy continues to inspire millions, proving that no obstacle is too great to overcome.

Tony Robbins is a world-renowned motivational speaker, author, and life coach, known for his transformative seminars and books. Born in 1960, he faced a challenging childhood marked by poverty and instability. Despite these hardships, Robbins became a self-made success, using his passion for personal development to help millions achieve their goals. His seminars, such as *Unleash The Power Within*, have empowered people to break through limiting beliefs and create lasting change in their lives. Tony has also worked with leaders, athletes, and entrepreneurs to enhance their performance. Through his work, Robbins has become a symbol of personal empowerment and positive change.

These powerful examples remind us of something important: *Pain is universal*, but how we choose to face it makes all the difference. Whether it's the financial struggles of Amitabh Bachchan, the emotional pain of Deepika Padukone, or the personal challenges of Priyanka Chopra, each of these individuals has faced real-life pain—and they've allowed that pain to teach them, mold them, and propel them toward a brighter future.

So, I ask you: What if, like these incredible people, you could embrace your pain, face it head-on, and use it to fuel your growth and success? Pain doesn't have to be a roadblock. It can be the very thing that pushes us toward our highest potential. What would your life look like if you chose to rise above your challenges, just like they did?

Your emotional reactions, your triggers, your body pain, and your illness are your guides.

Your emotional reactions and triggers are not obstacles—they are guides, pointing you toward the parts of yourself that need healing and understanding. Every time something upsets, frustrates, or overwhelms you, it's an opportunity to look within. Instead of resisting or suppressing these feelings, what if you leaned in and asked, *what is this trying to teach me?*

Triggers reveal unresolved emotions, past wounds, and limiting beliefs that are ready to be acknowledged and transformed. Have you ever noticed how certain situations or people stir intense emotions in you? That's your heart signaling where growth is needed. When you stop reacting impulsively and start observing, you turn emotional turbulence into self-awareness. Have you ever noticed how certain feelings or situations seem to push you out of your comfort zone? Instead of resisting, what if you saw them as opportunities for growth and self-reflection?

Your pains or illnesses aren't just physical discomforts—they often carry emotional or spiritual messages. Could it be that they're reflecting unresolved emotions, unhealed wounds, or suppressed stress? By listening to your body and your heart, you can learn what these signals are trying to teach you.

The key is self-reflection and self-discovery.

When you pause and ask, *what is this experience trying to show me?* You open the door to healing and transformation. By embracing these guides, you begin to understand yourself on a deeper level and unlock the path to true healing.

◆ What to reflect on:
• What emotions or situations tend to trigger strong reactions in you, and what might they be revealing?
• Have you ever noticed a connection between your physical pain or illness and unresolved emotions?
• How can you create space for self-

reflection to better understand the messages behind your emotional and physical experiences?

Here are some examples

Emotional Reaction Example:

Imagine you're in a conversation, and someone criticizes your work. Your immediate emotional reaction might be anger or defensiveness. You feel a rush of heat, your heart races, and you want to justify yourself. But, if you pause to reflect, you might realize that this reaction stems from a deep-seated fear of not being good enough or an experience of being judged harshly. This emotional reaction is a guide, showing you areas of your self-worth that need healing.

Trigger Example:

Let's say you're in a group setting, and someone comments on how disorganized the team is. You feel irritated or uncomfortable, even though the comment wasn't directly aimed at you. This could be a trigger that brings up memories of past experiences where you felt criticized or unsupported. This trigger can guide you to reflect on your need for validation or control in situations, allowing you to examine why you react so strongly to certain words or situations.

Both emotional reactions and triggers invite you to explore deeper layers within yourself and offer valuable opportunities for growth through self-reflection.

Pain Example:

Let's say you're experiencing persistent lower back pain. You may notice that it worsens during stressful times, especially when you're feeling overwhelmed by responsibilities or pressure from your safety, survival, children, money, and home issues. This pain could be linked to emotional tension around burdens or a feeling of being unsupported. Lower back pain is often associated with feelings of financial stress or carrying the weight of life's demands. This could be a trigger for you to explore deeper feelings about your sense of security, and self-worth, or the emotional strain of feeling like you're doing everything alone.

Similarly, middle back pain can be connected to feelings of guilt or lack of emotional support, and neck pain might indicate stubbornness or difficulty in expressing yourself. These physical symptoms are guides to uncover emotional imbalances that need healing.

Each of these pains presents an opportunity for you to reflect on what might be happening internally and what emotional patterns may need to be released to bring balance to both your mind and body. They encourage you to tune into the body's whispers, as these sensations invite a deeper connection with your emotions and healing journey.

Illness examples

In metaphysical healing, illness is not just seen as a physical problem but as a reflection of emotional imbalances or unresolved inner conflicts. By addressing the emotional roots of these illnesses — whether it's repressed anger (cancer), heartbreak (heart disease), or self-rejection (autoimmune diseases)—individuals can begin the healing process, aligning their mind, body, and spirit to restore health. Healing comes through emotional release, self-reflection, and cultivating positive energy, ultimately leading to a deeper sense of wholeness and wellness.

It's important to recognize that these metaphysical explanations are based on a holistic approach and are just one perspective on the potential emotional and psychological factors that may contribute to illness. Each person's journey is unique, and many factors—such as genetics, environment, lifestyle, and personal history—can influence the development of physical conditions. The mind-body connection is a powerful tool in healing, but it's crucial to approach it with a balanced view and consider other factors as well. These insights should be used as a guide, not a definitive explanation, and it's always recommended to consult medical professionals for a comprehensive approach to health and well-being.

1. Cancer

Metaphysical Understanding: Cancer is often seen in metaphysical terms as a reflection of deep emotional repression and unresolved inner conflict. It can stem from long-term suppressed emotions like anger, grief, resentment, undelivered communications, bitterness, or fear that are not expressed or processed. These repressed feelings create energetic blockages that prevent the body's natural healing processes from flowing freely, resulting in the growth of abnormal cells.

The metaphysical perspective suggests that cancer occurs when the body's natural healing abilities are overwhelmed by the emotions that have been held inside for too long. These emotions create disharmony in the energetic field, and if left unaddressed, they manifest physically as tumors or cellular mutations. For example, the breast is associated with issues around nurturing and self-care, and lung cancer may relate to grief and sorrow.

2. Heart Disease

Metaphysical Understanding: Heart disease is often linked to emotional heart wounds such as heartbreak, betrayal, or unresolved grief. From a metaphysical perspective, the heart chakra—which governs love, compassion, and emotional well-being—becomes blocked when individuals have difficulty processing emotions related to love, self-worth, or acceptance. Prolonged stress or feelings of fear and helplessness can cause the energetic heart to become congested, leading to physical manifestations of heart disease.

Heart disease may also reflect a lack of self-love or a stagnation in emotional flow. Individuals with heart issues often struggle with feeling unloved or unappreciated, whether in their relationships or their connection with themselves. Unexpressed emotions, especially around anger or resentment, can also weaken the heart, leading to physical manifestations such as high blood pressure or artery blockage.

3. Autoimmune Diseases

Metaphysical Understanding: Autoimmune diseases, in a metaphysical context, are thought to occur when the body's immune system attacks itself, often as a result of inner conflict or feelings of self-rejection. These diseases represent a disconnection from self—a struggle to accept or love oneself fully. People with autoimmune conditions may have subconscious beliefs of unworthiness or unresolved emotions of guilt or shame that lead to dissonance between the mind and body.

Emotional stress, trauma, or unresolved anger can trigger an energetic imbalance that causes the immune system to attack healthy cells. These emotional wounds often stem from childhood trauma, feeling unsupported, or carrying a deep sense of injustice. The underlying issue is often a lack of self-acceptance, where the person may feel like they are in a constant battle with themselves, mirroring the autoimmune process.

Please note, that the illness is more than what I have understood in metaphysics.

Emotions hide in some corners of your organ. So, simply, now I ask you: What emotional burden are you carrying that is showing up in your body?
What part of your life needs healing, whether it's around security, love, responsibility, or communication? Your body has been trying to tell you something, and it's time to listen to those whispers before they turn into louder messages.

What could you release, let go of, or shift so that your body can start to heal?

Think about it: Have you been holding onto anger or frustration? Is there something you've been avoiding in your life? Is there a situation that you feel is "choking" your ability to move forward or express yourself freely? Is there something you have been holding your thought process too rigid? These physical pains could be asking you to look deeper, to understand what emotions or beliefs are creating the discomfort.

My personal story of pain

For me, my journey of healing started with 18 years of knee pain that never seemed to go away, even after surgery. It was paining before surgery for three months and after surgery for 18 years. It was frustrating and exhausting. I tried everything to cure it, but nothing seemed to work. What I didn't realize at the time was that the pain wasn't just physical—it was tied to deeper, unresolved emotional pain. Then I started my journey to discover myself through learning many healing modalities.

I realized, the healing happened when I addressed my emotional wounds that I began to truly heal, when I realized my shadow side, my inner emotional wounds, my fears. The knee pain was a reflection of something deeper within me—years of suppressing feelings, of people-pleasing, of not giving myself the care and attention I needed. Once I recognized that, I began to focus on healing my emotional pain, and that's when I saw real change.

The emotional work I did allowed my body to finally start releasing the physical pain that had been trapped for so long. I realized that healing isn't just about addressing the symptoms—it's about going deeper and understanding the connection between the mind, body, and soul. When I healed emotionally, the physical pain followed.

Now, I look back and understand how much of my physical pain was connected to my emotional world. It wasn't just about my knee—it was about all the emotional burdens I had been carrying. It was a reminder that healing isn't always about what we see on the surface; sometimes, it's about what's hidden beneath.

So, I ask myself: What areas of my life are still in need of emotional healing? What physical discomfort might be connected to unresolved emotional wounds? And how can I continue to heal from the inside out? This journey has shown me that when I focus on emotional healing, everything else has the potential to fall into place.

What I've learned from my journey and in helping others is that our body's pain is rarely just physical. It's always connected to something emotional, something deeper. By tuning in to these pains, rather than just masking them with medication or ignoring them, we can start to address the root causes and find real healing. I had embarrassed my emotional wounds, my weakness, my vulnerabilities, my fears and I did make some efforts and actions to improve myself and that's how I managed to let go of the pain.

So, I ask you: What's your body trying to tell you? What is the illness you have?

Are there unresolved emotions that need to be looked at? What are the core thoughts or feelings behind your aches and pains? What are the emotional wounds and beliefs behind your illness?

When you start to listen, you'll be amazed at what you uncover. I have helped myself come out from knee pain, fibromyalgia, and thyroid.

While writing this book, I went through gallbladder removal surgery. The stones that were found weren't causing much pain, but the doctor advised removing them before they could create further complications. The lesson I learned from this experience was that sometimes, we need to address issues before they become painful or disruptive. Just like in life, certain emotional or mental burdens may not seem urgent at first, but if left unaddressed, they can grow into larger problems. Proactively taking care of our well-being—whether physical, emotional, or spiritual—is essential for a healthier, more balanced life.

Gallbladder stones form due to an imbalance in bile composition, often caused by excess cholesterol, bilirubin, or reduced bile salts. Poor diet, high in unhealthy fats and low in fiber, can contribute to their formation. Lack of physical activity and dehydration can further slow bile flow, leading to stone formation.

From an emotional and metaphysical perspective, gallbladder stones are often linked to suppressed anger, resentment, and unresolved emotions, particularly related to control, decision-making, and bitterness. The gallbladder is associated with the ability to process and release emotions, and when feelings are repressed, they may crystallize into physical blockages. Being a healer and metaphysician, I have worked on myself from multiple perspectives — emotionally, mentally, and energetically. Yet, I am still attracted to this health issue. I always thought I had forgiven others and myself, I have dealt with suppressed anger and resentment, bitterness, unexpressed emotions, and old patterns. Healing is an ongoing process and happens at an emotional level involves forgiveness, emotional release, assertive expression, and embracing change to restore balance in the body and mind. Today I am a metaphysician healer transforming people's lives, overcoming their emotional pains and challenges by taking charge of their thoughts, emotions, perceptions, and energy.

The Heart's Language of Pain

Pain is a form of communication—a language of the heart. It's the heart's way of saying, "Look here, there's something you need to pay attention to." Whether it's a heartbreak that reveals emotional wounds, physical pain that highlights areas of your life where you're out of alignment, or mental anguish that shows where limiting beliefs are holding you back, pain carries a message.

Here's the thing: the heart's wisdom isn't always easy to access. Sometimes, it comes through pain, because that's the only way we'll pay attention. The louder the pain, the more intense the message. Pain asks us to slow down, listen, and reflect on what we're avoiding or suppressing.

Why does this happen? Because when we're in pain, we can no longer ignore the signals our body and heart are sending. The pain brings us face to face with what's out of balance, what needs healing, and what we've been neglecting.

Turning Pain into a Teacher

I know—it's not easy. It can feel overwhelming. But when we take the time to sit with our pain, to listen to it, and to allow ourselves to feel it fully, we can start to transform it. Pain, when processed consciously, can be a teacher, guiding us toward healing and wisdom.

How can you begin to transform pain into wisdom? Here are some steps to guide you:

1. Acknowledge the Pain

The first step is to acknowledge the pain, instead of denying or pushing it away. It's okay to feel the pain—it's not a sign of weakness but a sign of being human. By accepting it, you can begin to understand its message.

Reflection Exercise:
Ask yourself, "What is this pain trying to tell me?"
Sit with the feeling and let it speak to you. What do you need to learn from it?
Remember, sometimes pain doesn't make

sense immediately, but if you stay with it long enough, clarity will come.

2. Allow the Emotion to Flow

Once you acknowledge the pain, the next step is to let the emotions flow through you. Don't try to bottle them up or numb them. Feel them fully, and let them pass. Emotions are energy in motion, and when we allow them to move through us, they lose their power to control us.

Mindful Breathing Exercise:
Inhale deeply and exhale slowly. As you breathe, visualize the pain or emotion moving through your body, leaving space for healing. Imagine the pain dissolving, turning into light, warmth, or whatever feeling resonates with you.

3. Ask Your Heart What It Needs

Pain often arises because something in your life is out of alignment. When you experience pain, ask your heart what it needs in that moment. Is it more love, more time for self-care, more boundaries, or more healing? The heart holds the wisdom of what you need to move forward.

Heart Dialogue Exercise:
Sit in a quiet space and ask your heart, "What do you need right now?"
Close your eyes and listen. Trust the answers that come, no matter how subtle they may be. Sometimes, the heart may ask for rest, forgiveness, or a new perspective. Trust that your heart knows what's best for you.

4. Release What No Longer Serves You

Pain often arises when we're holding onto things that no longer serve us—old hurts, regrets, or toxic situations. Once you've connected with the pain and allowed yourself to feel it, the next step is to release it. Let go of the emotional baggage and stories that keep you stuck.

Releasing Exercise:
Write down what you are ready to let go of—whether it's a limiting belief, an old wound, or a toxic relationship. After you've written it down, symbolically release it by

tearing the paper, burning it, or letting it go in any way that feels healing to you.

5. See the Blessing in Disguise

While it's easy to see pain as something purely negative, try to shift your perspective and see it as a blessing in disguise. Pain can be a profound teacher, showing you where you need to grow, heal, and evolve. Look for the lessons in your pain, and trust that it's leading you toward something better.

Reflection Exercise:
Ask yourself, "How can I grow from this pain? What lesson is this pain teaching me?"
You might be surprised at the depth of wisdom you uncover. Pain can help you awaken to a new version of yourself—one that is stronger, wiser, and more compassionate.

The Heart Heals Through Pain

Pain doesn't have to be something that overwhelms or defines us. When we start to listen to the heart, it transforms our relationship with pain. It becomes a tool for growth, a pathway to deeper self-awareness, and a guide to healing.

Remember this: The heart can heal what the mind cannot. The heart knows how to turn pain into power, fear into courage, and suffering into wisdom. You are capable of transmuting your pain into something beautiful, something that can propel you into your next chapter of life with more love, clarity, and understanding.

The next time you experience pain, remember that it is not your enemy. It is your teacher, guiding you toward a deeper connection with yourself and your heart's wisdom.

Are you ready to listen to the secrets that pain has to offer?

How to synchronize head and heart

When it comes to situations that threaten our safety, security, and survival, the connection between the head and heart becomes essential. This unity is critical because it helps us make quick, effective decisions that are not just emotionally driven but also grounded in reality. Let's break this down and explore how this synchronization works.

Heart and Mind Reacting Together

Real example situation: Boss Fires You

Imagine you walk into your boss's office, and they unexpectedly fire you. In that moment, you experience a surge of emotions—shock, fear, anxiety, and perhaps even anger. At the same time, your mind races to process the situation: "What do I do now?", "How will I pay my bills?", and "What's next for me?"

Fear Response (Heart)

The moment your boss delivers the news, your heart rate spikes, and you feel a rush of adrenaline. Your sympathetic nervous system is activated because your brain perceives this as a threat to your survival. The fear is real. Your heart pumps faster to prepare for an immediate fight-or-flight response.

Mental Processing (Head)

At the same time, your brain processes the information rapidly. It might be in shock, trying to make sense of the event, or it may immediately jump into problem-solving mode. Thoughts like, "What went wrong?", "How can I fix this?", and "What are my options?" rush in. This is the brain's way of trying to restore a sense of control, even if the situation feels out of your hands.

How Synchronizing the Heart and Mind Helps in These Moments:

To effectively respond, you need to find a way to synchronize your emotions (heart) and rational thoughts (head). Here's how this can work:

1. Ground Yourself in the Moment

The first step is to pause before reacting. Take a few deep breaths, slow your heart rate, and allow your brain a moment to reset. This helps you break the cycle of panic or impulse. In stressful situations, we can often say things or make decisions we later regret. By calming both the heart and the mind, you create space for more thoughtful responses.

◆ Action Tip:

Before you speak or react, take 3 deep breaths. Feel your heart rate slow and let the oxygen fill your brain, giving you clarity. Ask yourself, "What is the best course of action right now?"

2. Honor Your Emotions, Then Reframe Your Thoughts

Your heart will feel fear, anger, or sadness because your survival instincts are triggered. Honor these emotions—they are a natural part of the process. But then, use your mind to reframe the situation. Ask yourself:

"What is this opportunity teaching me?"

"What can I do to turn this situation into something better?"

"How can I use my skills and knowledge to move forward?"

When the mind and heart align, your emotional clarity allows you to think more creatively about your next steps, rather than being paralyzed by fear or anger.

3. Take Action Based on Both Insight and Intuition

Once you've taken a moment to breathe, assess your emotions, and calm your thoughts, it's time to act. The heart offers intuition—what feels right—and the head guides you with practical reasoning. When synchronized, they allow you to take actions that are authentic and grounded in reality.

◆ Action Tip:

Identify the next step:

Start by updating your resume or LinkedIn profile.

Reflect on what you could learn from the situation to improve for your next opportunity.

Maybe this is a chance to explore a passion or side project you've been putting off.

4. Trust the Process and Let Go of Control

The moment you realize you can't control everything, trust that your heart and mind will guide you to where you need to go. If the firing was unfair, your heart may want to seek justice, but your mind knows that certain things are out of your control. Acceptance becomes a powerful tool. You've been through tough situations before, and you can rise again. This is the resilience of the heart and mind working together.

5. Self-Compassion in the Process

Your heart also encourages self-compassion. It's easy to fall into self-criticism and shame after such a blow, but it's important to speak kindly to yourself. Reflect on what you've accomplished so far and trust that this situation doesn't define you. Your heart intelligence reminds you that this is just one chapter in your story, and there's always room for a fresh start.

◆ Action Tip:

Write down positive affirmations to remind yourself of your strengths:

"I am capable."

"I trust my ability to grow through challenges."

"I am worthy of success."

Benefits of Synchronizing Your Head and Heart:

Calmness: You stay grounded, reducing the likelihood of rash decisions driven by fear or anger.

Clarity: Your heart will guide you to what feels right, while your head will help you figure out the logistics.

Empowerment: You make decisions that are aligned with both your intuition and rational thinking, empowering you to take control.

Resilience: Through this process, you can quickly bounce back from setbacks because you've tapped into both emotional wisdom and logical thinking.

Final Thought:

In moments of crisis, such as being fired, synchronizing the head and heart isn't just helpful—it's essential. It's the bridge between survival mode and flourishing. When the mind and heart work together, you can move from a state of panic to a state of empowered action. Trust yourself, trust the process, and know that you have the tools within you to navigate any storm that comes your way.

Healing Through Pain

Pain is one of life's most difficult emotions to navigate. Yet, paradoxically, it often holds the key to profound healing. It is through pain that we are invited to look deeper into ourselves, to uncover truths that we might otherwise overlook. By processing pain mindfully and compassionately, we can unlock its wisdom, transform our suffering, and heal.

But how do we heal through pain? How do we process and uncover the lessons that pain brings? Below are several powerful

methods that can guide you through this journey of healing.

1. Journaling: The Power of Written Reflection

Journaling can be a transformative tool when it comes to processing pain. Writing down your thoughts and emotions allows you to externalize them and gain clarity. It also helps you express things you may not even realize you're feeling—things that may be buried deep within.

Why It Works: Journaling helps you create a safe space for your emotions to be heard, without judgment or limitation. It encourages reflection, understanding, and self-discovery. By getting your thoughts onto paper, you allow your heart and mind to process what's happening inside.

Journaling Exercise for Healing Pain:

Start with Your Pain: Write about what's causing you pain. How does it feel? What are the emotions attached to it—anger, sadness, confusion, fear? Let yourself write freely, without worrying about grammar or structure.

Ask the Pain What It Wants: Ask your heart what the pain needs you to know. Write down the first thing that comes to mind. It could be a hidden fear, a lesson, or something you're avoiding.

Release Through Writing: Write a letter to the pain, as if you're speaking directly to it. Express everything you need to say—anger, frustration, fear, or even gratitude. Let it all out.

End with Healing: Conclude by writing about the lessons you've learned from this pain. How is it helping you grow? What has it taught you? What can you do to move forward to heal?

Journaling helps you release pent-up emotions and find clarity. It can be your sacred space for emotional release and insight.

2. Breathwork

Breathwork is an effective exercise to release stored emotions and stress from the body. By focusing on deep, mindful breathing, you can activate your parasympathetic nervous system, reducing stress and promoting relaxation. This practice helps you to ground yourself, clear stagnant emotions, and reconnect with your body, which is essential for healing from pain—whether emotional or physical. A simple breathwork exercise such as the 4-7-8 technique (inhale for 4 seconds, hold for 7 seconds, exhale for 8 seconds) can calm the mind and alleviate emotional tension.

3. Meditation & Visualization

Meditation helps to bring awareness to the present moment and cultivate a peaceful mindset. Through visualization, you can imagine releasing pain and negative energy from your body. You may visualize the pain leaving your body as light or energy, helping you create space for healing. Meditation helps to quiet the mind, allowing you to connect with your inner wisdom and gain insights into how to move forward from the pain.

Together, journaling, breathwork, and meditation form a holistic approach to healing. These practices help you express, release, and ultimately shift the energy of your pain, allowing you to move toward peace and recovery.

◆ What to reflect on:
• How do you currently process pain— mentally, emotionally, or physically?
• Have you tried breathwork or meditation to help release emotional tension? How did it feel?
• What impact might journaling have on your ability to heal from emotional pain?

Chapter 3

Truth 3: The Heart Holds Emotional Memory & Influences Your Thoughts and Emotions

Have you ever noticed how certain situations, even years later, can evoke a flood of emotions? Maybe a particular scent, sound, or memory from childhood can make your heart race or your mood shift, almost as if the emotion is still fresh. What if I told you that these emotions are not just abstract feelings, but are stored within your heart? That's right—the heart holds emotional memory.

But how does this work? How do past emotions continue to shape our present thoughts, actions, and reactions? And most importantly, how can we begin to release these emotional imprints to live more freely and authentically?

The Heart Holds Emotional Memory

Did you know your heart isn't just the center of love and connection? It's also the keeper of your emotional memories, storing every feeling and experience that shapes the way you perceive and respond to the world. These memories are not only stored in your mind but are deeply embedded within your heart, influencing how you react in your present life. Have you ever walked into a room and suddenly felt a heavy emotion, even though nothing in the moment triggered it? Or have you heard a song and been transported back in time, with a wave of emotion? Those feelings didn't come out of nowhere—they're the emotional imprints left by past experiences, stored in the vast reservoir of your heart.

Your heart is like an emotional vault. It holds both joyful moments and painful experiences, each leaving a trace. Every single moment, whether joyous or sorrowful, is imprinted within your heart. These emotional imprints are carried in your heart and subconscious mind, shaping your behaviors, reactions, and even your relationships. Have you noticed that certain situations or people trigger strong emotions? It's not just a coincidence; it's your heart and subconscious mind working together, reminding you of past lessons or unresolved wounds.

Here's where it gets interesting: Your subconscious mind is like the vast, hidden part of you that stores everything you've experienced. It holds onto emotional memories, even if you aren't consciously aware of them. These imprints are linked directly to your heart's intelligence, creating an intricate web that influences how you react today. When something triggers an emotion, it's often because your subconscious mind is bringing that past emotional memory up to the surface. These emotional patterns are not just random— they're guided by your heart and subconscious mind's deep-rooted connection.

But what if your heart and subconscious mind are holding onto negative memories— pain, trauma, or unhealed wounds? These can weigh you down, limiting how you experience life. Your heart may feel heavy with past emotions, and your subconscious mind can guide you toward repeating old patterns without you even realizing it. Have you ever tried to move forward, only to feel stuck by something from the past? That's your heart and subconscious holding onto unresolved emotions, blocking you from embracing the present.

Healing happens when we connect with both our heart and subconscious mind. By understanding that your heart's emotional memories are connected to your subconscious mind, you can start transforming those old wounds. When we acknowledge these emotional imprints, we unlock the power to rewrite the story. Your subconscious mind isn't set in stone. It can be rewired, just like your heart's memory can be healed. Have you ever felt a deep, instinctive knowing about something, like you just "knew" what was right for you? That's your heart and subconscious mind working together, guiding you toward healing.

Ask yourself:

Can you recall a moment where an emotion you felt came from a memory stored deep within you, in your heart or subconscious mind?

Are there patterns in your life that repeat themselves, despite your efforts to break free? What might your subconscious mind be holding onto from the past?

How do you feel when you think about certain memories? Does your heart feel light or heavy, and how does your subconscious mind influence those feelings?

Healing emotional memories involves understanding that your heart and subconscious mind are in constant communication. When you're triggered by something, it's often your subconscious mind pulling up old emotional imprints from your heart. To heal, you must not only acknowledge these memories but also let go of them, so they no longer shape your present or future.

Reflection:

What emotional reactions have shaped the way you feel about certain situations or people? Can you trace those feelings back to an experience stored in your heart or subconscious mind?

How does your heart react in various situations? Does it feel open, closed, light, or heavy? What might it be trying to tell you about past emotional experiences?

Are there emotions or memories that are still affecting you today? How can you start releasing them from both your heart and subconscious mind?

Action: Take a moment to connect with both your heart and subconscious mind. Place your hand over your chest and breathe deeply. Allow yourself to become present in the moment, feeling your heart's energy.

Ask yourself: What emotional memories might my heart and subconscious mind be holding onto?

Are there any memories that feel unresolved or heavy? Recognize these emotions, and gently acknowledge them without judgment. When you're ready, invite healing energy into your heart and mind.

Say to yourself: "I release the past and open myself to healing." Feel the shift within you, as you let go of emotional baggage stored in your heart and subconscious mind.

By understanding that your heart and subconscious mind are both powerful sources of wisdom, you can begin to heal and transform your emotional landscape. They hold the key to unlocking emotional freedom and embracing a life full of peace, joy, and possibility.

Are you ready to set your heart and subconscious mind free?

Let's dive into this powerful concept and understand how our heart's emotional memory influences our thoughts and emotions.

The Concept of Emotional Memory Stored in the Heart

Emotional memory refers to the feelings and experiences that are encoded in your body and heart throughout your life. It's as if your heart keeps a record of every significant emotional event you've experienced, from joyful moments to moments of hurt, grief, or trauma. These emotional memories don't just exist in the mind; they reside deeply in your heart, influencing not just how you feel, but also how you react to situations and people.

Why is this important?
Your heart doesn't just store memories; it remembers the emotional experience tied to those memories. For example, if you experienced betrayal in the past, your heart may still carry that hurt, even if the event happened years ago. When something in the present triggers a similar emotion— perhaps an innocent comment or an unexpected action—you may find yourself reacting with unexpected intensity or defensiveness. This is an emotional memory at work.

Emotional memory influences not only how we feel but also how we think. Our heart's emotional imprint creates patterns in the brain that influence thoughts and beliefs about ourselves, the world, and others. It's why some people develop trust issues or low self-esteem after experiencing emotional pain—it's not just a mental decision but a heart-based emotional reaction that keeps influencing thoughts and behaviors.

How Emotional Memory Shapes Thought Patterns

Our heart's emotional memory isn't just an archive of past pain; it actively shapes how we interpret the world today. Let's break down how this works.

Emotional Triggers: Have you ever been in a situation where a seemingly harmless comment triggered an intense emotional reaction—maybe anger, sadness, or fear? This is often due to emotional triggers— specific words, actions, or situations that resonate with unresolved emotional memories. These triggers can cause you to react impulsively as if the original emotional memory has been "reactivated," even if the current situation doesn't justify such an intense response.

Example: A person who experienced abandonment in childhood may find themselves overreacting in adult relationships when they feel ignored or neglected, even if their partner's actions aren't intentionally hurtful. The heart's emotional memory of abandonment amplifies the present experience, causing an emotional reaction that might seem disproportionate to the situation.

Thought Patterns and Beliefs: The emotions stored in the heart have a way of influencing how we think. For example, someone who has experienced rejection might develop negative thoughts about their worth, believing "I am unlovable" or "I am not good enough." These thought patterns are deeply tied to the heart's emotional memory. Over time, they shape how you perceive yourself and others.

The heart, holding these emotions, has a way of shaping our perception of reality, sometimes allowing us to create the right interpretations or sometimes twisted. If you've experienced pain in the past, your heart might filter current experiences through the lens of that pain, distorting your thoughts, beliefs, and emotions. The heart's wisdom—when untapped—can create cognitive biases that limit your ability to connect with others and make empowered decisions. It stops you from being loving and lovable. It stops you from creating meaningful connections in relations.

Emotional Memory's Impact on Emotional Reactions

Our heart's emotional memory can create an emotional echo—a resonance from past experiences that colors our present emotions. Here are a few ways this can impact your emotional responses:

Repeated Emotional Reactions: When we are unaware of the emotional memories stored in our hearts, we often repeat the same emotional reactions over and over. For instance, if you've been hurt in the past by someone's criticism, your heart may "remember" the pain associated with judgment and trigger a defensive or angry reaction when faced with similar criticism in the present.

These patterns can become automatic, and over time, they reinforce the idea that you are always vulnerable to emotional pain. Without recognizing the underlying emotional memory, you might continue reacting in the same way—without understanding the deeper source.

Emotional Overwhelm: Sometimes, when old emotional memories rise to the surface, they can feel overwhelming. You may find yourself crying or feeling anxious without a clear reason. This emotional flood may not even be related to the present situation but is often an accumulation of unresolved emotions from the past.

It's not uncommon for someone to feel emotionally "stuck" or perpetually overwhelmed by emotions that seem to have no explanation. However, these feelings can often be traced back to unresolved emotional memories held in the heart.

Increased Sensitivity: Emotional memories can also increase your sensitivity to similar situations. For example, if you've been emotionally hurt by someone, your heart may become more sensitive to certain behaviors that trigger that past pain. You may find yourself overreacting to small actions or words that remind you of the original hurt, creating a cycle of emotional sensitivity that affects your relationships.

Healing the Heart's Emotional Memory

Understanding that emotional memory is stored in the heart is the first step to healing it. But how do you begin to unravel the emotional imprints from the past and create space for healing?

Here are some healing practices to help you release emotional memories that no longer serve you:

Mindfulness and Self-Awareness: Mindfulness helps you stay present and aware of your emotions in the moment. When you can observe your reactions and thought patterns without judgment, you can begin to separate the current situation from the emotional memory stored in your heart.

Exercise: When you feel triggered, take a deep breath and pause. Acknowledge that the emotion you're feeling might not be entirely about the present moment. Reflect on where this emotion may have originated from and how it might be linked to past experiences. Permit yourself to feel without attaching to the old memory.

Forgiveness and Compassion for self and others:
Often, emotional memories are tied to past hurts, whether caused by others or by ourselves. Healing comes when we forgive—not just the person who hurt us, but also ourselves for holding onto the pain for so long.

Exercise: Practice saying, "I forgive myself for holding onto this pain," and "I forgive others for any harm they may have caused." This practice of forgiveness is a powerful way to clear your heart and mind of past wounds.

I love this simple method 'The *Ho'oponopono'* it is truly powerful in its simplicity. It offers a beautiful way to release emotional burdens and heal memories by cultivating compassion, not just for others but for ourselves too. The four lines—*I'm sorry. Please forgive me. Thank you. I Love You*—is a reminder of the deep healing that can occur when we take responsibility for our emotions, our reactions, and our energy.

By saying these words, we acknowledge our role in the energy exchanges we've had, whether we were conscious of it or not, whether it happened in this life or past life. It's a form of self-compassion, where we forgive ourselves for holding on to negative patterns or past mistakes, and we also offer that forgiveness to others. When we say "I'm sorry," we're acknowledging that pain exists, and when we say "Please forgive me," we're letting go of guilt and shame. The phrase "Thank you" brings gratitude into the equation, creating space for healing and release. You are being compassionate to yourself, and finally, "I love you" reminds us of our innate worth, of the love we should always offer to ourselves and others, regardless of circumstances. It's simple yet profound, transforming emotional and energetic blocks into opportunities for deep healing and forgiveness.

Releasing Stored Emotions with the help of EFT

We all carry emotional baggage—old hurts, unhealed wounds, past experiences—that often shape the way we navigate life. These emotions become stored in the heart and can influence everything from how we react to everyday situations to how we see ourselves. The beauty is that you don't have to carry these burdens forever. There are powerful tools available to help release the emotional baggage stored in your heart, so you can live with more peace, joy, and freedom.

This practical technique EFT - Emotional Freedom Technique, is simple and easy to use, it unlocks and heals the heart's stored memories, allowing you to create space for new, empowering emotions to flow through your being.

Emotional Freedom Technique (EFT) EFT, also known as tapping, is a powerful and effective technique that helps to release stored emotions and negative beliefs. By tapping on specific meridian points on the body, you can help to break down the emotional charge that is linked to memories, releasing pent-up emotions, and restoring a sense of balance. I still suggest you learn from experts and get trained well, rather than carrying an opinion that EFT does not work.

How EFT works:

The concept behind EFT is simple: when we experience negative emotions, the energy in our body becomes blocked. This blockage is what can cause distress and discomfort. By tapping on certain meridian points, you restore the energy flow, allowing emotions to release and clear out the stagnation.

Steps for EFT Practice:

Identify the emotion: What feeling or memory are you holding onto? It might be pain, anger, fear, or sadness. Tune into it.

Rate the intensity: On a scale of 0 to 10, how intense is the emotion? This helps you track your progress as you tap.

The Setup Statement: While tapping on the "karate chop" point (side of the hand), repeat a phrase like, "Even though I feel [emotion], I deeply and completely accept myself."

Tap on meridian points: Tap each of the following points while focusing on your emotion:

1. Top Of The Head
2. Eyebrow
3. Side Of The Eye
4. Under The Eye
5. Under The Nose
6. Chin
7. Collarbone
8. Under The Arm

As you tap, repeat a reminder phrase like, "I'm releasing this [emotion] from my heart now."

Re-assess intensity: After a round of tapping, reassess how the emotion feels. You may find the intensity has reduced. Repeat as needed until the emotion dissipates.

EFT is an incredibly effective tool to clear away old emotional patterns stored in your heart, enabling you to feel lighter, more empowered, and more in touch with your true self.

For example, EFT can be particularly effective in releasing tough emotions, such as deep grief or betrayal, which often feel heavy and hard to move past. Let's take the example of grief from losing a loved one. Sometimes, the sadness can be overwhelming, and no matter how much we try to "move on," the pain seems to linger.

Here's an example of how you can use EFT to release grief: for reference to diagrams, you may find EFT tapping diagram images on Google.

Example EFT for Releasing Grief:

Identify the Emotion:

"I feel a deep sense of loss and sadness about the passing of my loved one. It feels like a weight on my chest, and it's hard to breathe freely."

Rate the Intensity:

On a scale of 0 to 10, you might rate your grief as a 9 or 10 in intensity.

Setup Statement:

While tapping on the karate chop point (side of the hand), say:

"Even though I feel this deep grief and sadness from the loss of my loved one, I deeply and completely accept myself."

Tap on Meridian Points:

Tap on each of the following points, while repeating a reminder phrase that focuses on your emotion of grief:

Top of the Head: "This grief is overwhelming."

Eyebrow: "I miss them so much."

Side of the Eye: "I feel a heavy sadness in my heart."

Under the Eye: "It's so hard to let go of the pain."

Under the Nose: "I don't know how to move on."

Chin: "I carry this sadness within me."

Collarbone: "This grief feels like it's never-ending."

Under the Arm: "I want to release this sadness and find peace."

Re-assess Intensity:

After one round of tapping, stop and reassess how you feel.

Do you feel lighter? Is the intensity of your grief less? Maybe it's now a 6 or 7 instead of a 10. If you still feel the grief strongly, repeat the tapping process. Or do it every day till the intensity is zero.

You can add variations to the reminder phrase as per your understanding and feelings such as: "I'm ready to heal this sadness," or "I release the tightness in my heart and allow myself to find peace."

Emotional Benefits:
By doing this tapping process, you allow your body to process and release some of

the stuck energy tied to grief. It won't ease the pain of the loss, but it can help to lessen the intensity of the emotion, making it easier to cope and eventually find more peace and acceptance.

Do you know?

The human adult body has approximately 37.2 trillion cells and around 86 billion neurons. The constant interaction between these cells and neurons facilitates communication throughout the body, including the processing and storage of emotional memories.

Our emotional memory is primarily stored in the limbic system, a complex network of structures in the brain responsible for emotions, memory, and arousal. Key areas such as the amygdala, hippocampus, and hypothalamus play a central role in processing and storing emotional experiences. These emotions become imprinted not only in the brain but also in the body's cells, affecting both our mental and physical well-being. When these emotional wounds remain unaddressed, they can manifest as chronic pain, stress, or illness. Healing emotional wounds requires deep emotional processing, self-reflection, and conscious effort to release these memories. As a mindset healer and coach, I suggest practices such as journaling, mindfulness, meditation, EFT, Chakra Balancing, breathwork, and therapeutic techniques, one can begin to shift these stored emotions, allowing us to heal and restore balance, ultimately freeing ourselves from the burden of past trauma.

Additionally, the heart is said to produce a stronger electromagnetic field than the brain. It is estimated that the heart's electromagnetic field can be up to 60 times greater in amplitude than the brains, and it plays a significant role in influencing our emotions, intuition, and overall well-being. The heart's wisdom, in many ways, is a powerful source of guidance for emotional healing and self-awareness.

The solution lies in holding the heart's intelligence and using its wisdom to create a life of balance, health, and purpose. By tuning into the heart, we can access deeper emotional awareness, connect to our true desires, and navigate our lives with clarity and compassion.

Using the heart's intelligence, we can improve health, enhance relationships, discover purpose, live and an authentic life. By integrating the heart's wisdom into our daily lives, we create a powerful foundation for holistic well-being and purpose-driven living.

For me, learning is growing. I constantly expand my understanding through books and workshops and these resources have deeply influenced my journey. These five books are a treasure to the mind.

The Biology of Belief by Dr. Bruce Lipton explains that our beliefs shape our biology, influencing gene expression and health. Negative or limiting beliefs can cause stress, leading to illness, while positive beliefs can promote healing. The mind-body connection shows that our perceptions and thoughts significantly impact our physical reality, and by changing our beliefs, we can align with the body's natural ability to heal.

You Can Heal Your Life by Louise Hay emphasizes the power of affirmations and self-talk in healing. Negative self-talk and unresolved emotions contribute to physical ailments. By practicing self-love, forgiveness, and positive affirmations, we can heal emotional wounds and change patterns, allowing the body to heal itself. The book teaches that emotional healing is key to overall well-being.

"Redikall Crystalline Mind" by Aatmn, my mentor is a powerful guide to unlocking the potential of the mind and consciousness. It explores the process of reprogramming limiting beliefs and old thought patterns, offering a clear path to elevate one's awareness and vibrational frequency. The book delves into the concept of crystalline clarity, teaching how to achieve mental clarity, emotional healing, and heightened spiritual awareness. By understanding and applying these principles, readers can shift their energy and consciousness to create profound transformation. It's a valuable resource for anyone seeking to break free from past limitations and step into their true potential.

"Being You, Changing the World"
In this book, Dain Heer encourages readers to embrace their true selves, free from the limitations of societal expectations. It's about discovering who you are and how you can contribute to the world by being authentic and fully present. This book invites readers to embrace their uniqueness and authenticity. Dain Heer explores how stepping into who you truly are can change not only your life but also the world around you. It's a call to stop conforming to others' expectations and start living as your true self.

"The Generative Being"
Gary Douglas's books are filled with tools and insights that empower individuals to break free from limiting beliefs, step into their full potential, and create a life of ease and possibility. This book encourages people to tap into their innate generative ability to create their reality. It's about recognizing and cultivating the power

within to make changes in any area of life,
be it health, relationships, or career.

Chapter 4

*Truth 4: Your Heart Speaks to Your Body:
The Silent Language of Emotions & Health*

Have you ever noticed how stress, anxiety, or even unresolved emotions can affect your physical body? Perhaps you've experienced a tightness in your chest when anxious, a stomach ache when stressed, or a headache after a difficult conversation. These physical symptoms are not just random—they are the body's way of communicating with you. The connection between your heart's emotions and your physical health is profound, and understanding it is the key to unlocking a deeper level of well-being.

Our heart holds more than just emotions—it also communicates with our bodies, sending signals about the state of our mental, emotional, and physical health. In this truth section, we'll explore the heart-body connection and how your heart's wisdom can guide you toward greater health and balance.

Understanding the Heart-Body Conversation

The heart doesn't always speak in words—it communicates through sensations, feelings, and emotions that manifest in the body. Every part of your body can reflect the energy and emotions stored within the heart. These signals are like a secret language that can guide you toward healing, balance, and well-being.

Think about it: When you feel anxious or stressed, you may notice a tightness in your chest, shallow breathing, or tension in your shoulders. This is the body's way of reflecting what's happening in your heart. Conversely, when you experience joy, love, or peace, you may feel an expansive, light sensation in your chest or a sense of openness in your heart.

When you're about to face an exam, a presentation, or any situation that triggers fear or nervousness, your body responds in specific ways, often creating a sense of discomfort or physical sensations. One of the most common sensations is the "butterflies in the stomach." Here's how this happens:

The Body's Stress Response (Fight-or-Flight):

Fear activates the sympathetic nervous system, which is responsible for the "fight-or-flight" response. This is an evolutionary mechanism designed to prepare the body for action in times of perceived danger. The moment you experience fear, your body releases stress hormones like adrenaline and cortisol.

Changes in Digestion:

One of the body's responses to stress is to prioritize vital functions like muscle strength and quick reflexes, rather than digestion. This is why you might feel the sensation of butterflies in your stomach — it's due to reduced blood flow to the stomach and intestines, leading to a fluttery or uneasy feeling.

Increased Heart Rate and Breathing:
As part of the fight-or-flight response, your heart rate increases, and your breathing becomes quicker and shallower. This helps

to supply more oxygen to your muscles for quick action. You might feel your heart racing and your breath quickening when you're anxious or fearful about an exam.

Tension in the Body:
The muscles throughout your body, including those in the stomach, often become tense when you're afraid. You might feel a tightness or knot in your stomach or a clenched jaw. This physical tension is part of the body's instinct to prepare for a stressful situation.

Heightened Senses:
Fear sharpens your senses, making you more alert to your surroundings. This is why you may notice your senses becoming more acute during moments of fear—your body is preparing for any potential threats, even though, in an exam scenario, there may be no immediate physical danger.

These physical reactions are all part of how the body recognizes and responds to fear. The "butterflies" are just one example of how the body gives you sensory signals, informing you that you're experiencing fear or nervousness. The key to overcoming this fear is learning to manage your body's response through techniques like deep breathing, grounding exercises, or mindful awareness, which can help you calm your nervous system and reduce physical tension.

Listening to the Body

Have you ever wondered what your body is trying to tell you? Every ache, pain, or sensation in your body is a message from your heart—a communication that often goes unnoticed because we're too busy with the demands of the mind and life. But when we pause, tune in, and truly listen, we can decipher the messages our heart is sending us.

Our bodies are constantly in conversation with us. The physical sensations we experience are reflections of our emotional states. The key to deepening the connection between the heart and body is learning to listen to the body's signals. In this section, we'll explore how you can tune into your body to understand what your heart is trying to communicate.

Imagine this: Your heart is not just a physical organ that pumps blood. It is a center of intelligence, an energy source that is constantly communicating with your body. Every emotion, thoughts, and feelings you experience, is mirrored in the body, creating a dynamic system of signals and responses. When we suppress emotions or live in a state of stress, these unaddressed feelings eventually manifest as physical ailments.

But how does this work?

The Science Behind Emotions and the Body

When you experience an emotion — whether joy, anger, fear, or sadness — the brain triggers a series of physiological responses. For instance, fear can cause a rise in cortisol (the stress hormone), triggering a fight-or-flight response that elevates heart rate and blood pressure. Similarly, stress can cause muscle tension, digestive issues, and even chronic pain.

The heart, as the emotional center, is often at the core of these responses. It beats faster in moments of anxiety, flutters during moments of excitement, and can even feel "heavy" when experiencing sadness or grief.

When we ignore these emotional cues, we create a disconnect between the heart and the body. Over time, this disconnection can lead to physical symptoms such as fatigue, headaches, digestive problems, and even chronic conditions like heart disease.

How Emotions Manifest in the Body

Each emotion has a unique impact on the body, and understanding this can help you decipher the messages your heart is sending:

Anxiety and Stress: These emotions often manifest in the body as tightness in the chest, shallow breathing, heart palpitations, or tension in the neck and shoulders. Your heart races, signaling a fight-or-flight response.

Sadness and Grief: When we experience sorrow, the body may feel fatigued, heavy, or weighed down. You may feel an actual physical ache in your chest as if your heart is "broken."

Anger: Anger is often associated with increased blood pressure, headaches, and muscle tension. The heart may beat rapidly, signaling an emotional outburst or frustration.

Fear: Fear can make you feel cold, and your heart may race as it prepares for potential danger. This is your body's way of preparing for fight or flight.

Joy and Excitement: Positive emotions like happiness and excitement can cause your heart to feel light and full, expanding with warmth and energy.

The Power of Listening to the Body

What if your body is a mirror reflecting your emotional state? The key is to listen. By tuning into your heart and body, you can start to identify the emotions that are causing physical symptoms. For instance, if you frequently experience tightness in your chest, it might be a sign that you're holding onto unexpressed emotions such as grief, anger, or anxiety.

Have you ever wondered what your body is trying to tell you? Every ache, pain, or sensation in your body is a message from your heart—a communication that often goes unnoticed because we're too busy with the demands of the mind and life. But when we pause, tune in, and truly listen, we can decipher the messages our heart is sending us.

Our bodies are constantly in conversation with us. The physical sensations we experience are reflections of our emotional states. The key to deepening the connection between the heart and body is learning to listen to the body's signals. In this section, we'll explore how you can tune into your body to understand what your heart is trying to communicate.

When you learn to listen to your body, it becomes a powerful tool for emotional healing. The body, after all, is not working against you—it's simply sending you messages to help you take better care of yourself. Each ache, pain, or discomfort can be seen as an opportunity to check in with your heart and ask, "What do I need to release? What am I holding onto?"

Practical Tools for Healing the Heart-Body Connection

The good news is that the heart-body connection can be healed. By addressing both emotional and physical needs, you can restore balance and achieve greater well-being. Here are some practical tools to strengthen your heart-body connection:

1. Mindful Breathing

Breath is the bridge between your heart and body. When you consciously slow down your breath, you calm your nervous system, release stress, and help your heart return to a state of balance.

How to Practice Mindful Breathing:

Sit in a comfortable position, close your eyes, and take a deep breath through your nose.

As you inhale, visualize your breath flowing into your heart. Feel the energy of your heart expanding as it fills with warmth.

Exhale slowly through your mouth, releasing any tension or stress.

Focus on the rhythm of your breath. Continue this process for 5-10 minutes daily to calm your mind and body and strengthen your heart's connection.

Yes, the power of listening to the body and emotions is deeply connected with the practice of conscious breathing. Breathing serves as a bridge between the mind, body, and emotions, helping to create awareness and bring a sense of presence. By focusing on your breath, you can access deeper levels of understanding, allowing you to listen to and honor the signals your body and emotions are sending.

How Breathing Helps:

Grounding and Awareness – Slow, mindful breathing helps you stay present and aware of your body's sensations, allowing you to tune into the emotional and physical signals that arise.

Releasing Tension – Deep breathing activates the parasympathetic nervous system, helping to release tension and calm your body, making it easier to process and understand emotions.

Emotional Release – Breathing into areas of tension in your body can help release suppressed emotions, allowing healing energy to flow and supporting emotional balance.

Regulating Energy – Conscious breathing can help regulate your energy, bringing balance and harmony to both physical and emotional states, and guiding you through emotional turbulence.

Accessing Inner Wisdom – The breath is often a direct link to your inner self, and by tuning into it, you can access your intuition and wisdom to better understand your body's messages.

Through the power of breathing, you can foster a deeper connection with your body and emotions, promoting healing and self-awareness.

Here are 10 breathing hacks to help you manage different moods and emotional states:

1. For Anxiety: 4-7-8 Breathing

This technique helps calm the nervous system and is great for managing anxiety or feelings of overwhelm.

How to do it: Inhale through your nose for 4 counts, hold your breath for 7 counts, and exhale slowly through your mouth for 8 counts.

Why it works: The elongated exhalation activates the parasympathetic nervous system, which reduces stress and induces a feeling of calm.

2. For Stress Relief: Diaphragmatic Breathing

When stress hits, deep belly breathing is a powerful tool for grounding.

How to do it: Sit or lie down, place one hand on your chest and the other on your belly. Inhale deeply through your nose, allowing your belly to expand, and exhale fully through your mouth.

Why it works: It engages the diaphragm, slowing your heart rate and lowering cortisol levels. This breathing technique also helps shift the focus away from stressors and back into the body.

3. For Focus: Box Breathing (Square Breathing)

When you need clarity or concentration, box breathing is an excellent way to reset your mind.

How to do it: Inhale for 4 counts, hold for 4 counts, exhale for 4 counts, and hold for 4 counts. Repeat.

Why it works: This rhythm helps stabilize your breath, which calms your nervous system and enhances concentration. It provides structure to a chaotic mind.

4. For Fatigue: Stimulating Breath

When you're feeling sluggish or need a burst of energy, this breathing method helps rejuvenate you.

How to do it: Inhale and exhale through the nose rapidly, about 1-2 breaths per second, for 15-30 seconds.

Why it works: It stimulates the sympathetic nervous system, energizing the body and mind. This is akin to a "recharge" for your energy levels.

5. For Overwhelm: Alternate Nostril Breathing

If you feel emotionally scattered or out of balance, this technique restores harmony.

How to do it: Using your right thumb, close your right nostril. Inhale deeply through the left nostril, close the left nostril with your right ring finger, and exhale through the right nostril. Then inhale through the right nostril, close it, and exhale through the left nostril. Repeat.

Why it works: This practice balances both hemispheres of the brain, calming the nervous system and helping you regain a sense of grounded equilibrium.

6. For Grief or Sadness: Ocean's Breath (Ujjayi Pranayama)

When you're overwhelmed by sadness or grief, soothing, ocean-like breathing can ease emotional turbulence.

How to do it: Inhale deeply through your nose, and as you exhale, slightly constrict your throat to create a sound like ocean waves. Continue breathing in this manner for several minutes.

Why it works: The sound of the breath creates a calming, meditative effect, helping to release pent-up emotion and providing emotional relief.

7. For Anger: Extended Exhalation Breathing

If you're feeling triggered or irritated, controlling the exhalation can help calm intense emotions.

How to do it: Inhale deeply for 4 counts, then exhale slowly and steadily for 8-10 counts. Focus on lengthening the exhalation.

Why it works: A longer exhale signals to your body that it's safe to relax, which reduces the intensity of anger and gives you a moment to regain control.

8. For Happiness: Heart-Centered Breathing

When you feel joy, excitement, or gratitude, this technique helps you stay connected to your heart's energy.

How to do it: Place one hand on your heart and one on your belly. Inhale deeply through the nose, feeling your chest and heart area expand. Exhale gently through the mouth, letting go of any tension.

Why it works: Focusing on the heart area creates an emotional connection to joy and allows you to amplify positive feelings, enhancing the overall sense of well-being.

9. For Loneliness: Compassionate Breathing

When feeling lonely or disconnected, compassionate breathing helps create a sense of self-love and connection.

How to do it: Inhale deeply, imagining you're breathing in love and compassion for yourself. As you exhale, send that same love out to the world or to others you wish to connect with.

Why it works: This practice nurtures self-compassion, which counters feelings of isolation and fosters a deep connection with both self and the world around you.

10. For Calm Before Sleep: 3-Part Breathing

If you're struggling to sleep or relax, this breathing technique helps prepare the body for rest.

How to do it: Inhale through your nose and let the breath fill your belly, then expand the chest, and finally, feel the breath rise into the upper chest. Exhale slowly, starting from the upper chest, then the ribs, and finally the belly.

Why it works: This deep, full-body breath creates a relaxed state, activating the parasympathetic nervous system and signaling that it's time to rest and restore.

By consciously using these breathing techniques in different emotional states, you can regulate your nervous system, enhance mental clarity, and cultivate emotional balance, ultimately taking charge of your well-being and energy.

Isn't it simple? Will you try this?

Healing the Heart Through the Body

Remember, the body and heart are not separate entities—they are intricately connected. By learning to listen to the messages your heart sends to your body, you can create a harmonious relationship between your emotional and physical health. When you heal one, you heal the other.

So, the next time you feel physical discomfort, pause and ask yourself: What is my heart trying to tell me? The answers are waiting for you in the silent language of your body and heart.

Your heart speaks to you every day, guiding you toward greater health and harmony. Will you listen?

But how do we listen more deeply?
Being a mindset healer and coach, my work revolves around mindset, emotions, beliefs,

174

perceptions, and energy. In metaphysical healing, the connection between emotions and physical health is deeply intertwined. Each emotion can be seen as a form of energy that, when unresolved or repressed, can manifest as physical ailments in the body. Let's explore the metaphysical understanding of stress, anger, sadness, resentment, and emotional toxins and their impact on various organs:

1. Stress and the Heart:

Metaphysical View: Stress is often linked to a feeling of being overwhelmed, unsupported, or having too many responsibilities. The heart, symbolizing love, compassion, and emotional connection, can suffer from excessive stress when it feels unsupported or trapped.

Physical Impact: Chronic stress and emotional overload can cause damage to the heart and blood vessels, leading to conditions like high blood pressure, heart attacks, and arrhythmias. In metaphysical terms, when we suppress our feelings, especially when we feel unloved, unsupported, or constantly pressured, it can manifest in heart-related diseases.

Heart Attack: A sudden, intense heart attack is often linked to overwhelming stress, especially when feelings of frustration, fear, and a lack of emotional release are deeply rooted. The heart is a symbol of vitality and love, and when blocked by stress, it can lead to physical symptoms like heart attacks.

2. Anger and the Liver:

Metaphysical View: Anger is strongly associated with the liver in metaphysical healing. The liver is seen as the organ of transformation and cleansing. When you hold onto anger, resentment, or frustration, it causes internal toxicity, which is reflected in liver issues.

Physical Impact: Anger and pent-up rage can lead to liver conditions like cirrhosis, fatty liver, and hepatitis. The liver is also responsible for detoxifying the body, so when emotions like anger are not processed or expressed healthily, they create emotional toxins that accumulate in the liver, causing dysfunction.

Emotional Reasoning: When anger is not released, it becomes internalized and can cause resentment. The liver's job is to metabolize and "cleanse" — when this cleansing process is blocked by unresolved anger, it creates imbalances that affect both mental and physical health.

3. Sadness, Grief, and the Lungs:

Metaphysical View: The lungs are seen as the organs responsible for taking in new life and releasing the old, symbolizing both grief and the capacity to breathe in new emotional experiences. Sadness, grief, and loss are deeply connected to the lungs. They hold the energy of sorrow and mourning.

Physical Impact: Chronic sadness and grief can manifest as respiratory issues such as asthma, bronchitis, chronic obstructive pulmonary disease (COPD), or even pneumonia. The emotional suppression of grief can prevent the body from "letting go" and "breathing in" new emotional experiences, leading to physical discomfort in the lungs.

Emotional Reasoning: When you refuse to release sadness or avoid facing grief, you create emotional blockages. The lungs become burdened with this unexpressed sorrow, which makes it difficult for you to "breathe freely" or embrace new beginnings.

4. Resentment and Kidney Stones:

Metaphysical View: The kidneys are thought to represent the filtering and cleansing of emotions. Resentment, bitterness, and holding onto old grudges are strongly linked with kidney dysfunction. When we refuse to forgive or let go of past hurts, it causes emotional toxicity that affects the kidneys.

Physical Impact: The metaphysical belief is that unresolved resentment creates tension and "grit" in the body, which can manifest physically as kidney stones. These stones are the body's attempt to crystallize these negative emotions, forming blocks that can prevent the natural flow of energy and life force.

Emotional Reasoning: Holding onto unresolved feelings, especially from long-standing emotional wounds, can create energetic blockages that manifest physically in the kidneys as stones, cysts, or other disorders.

5. Failure to Release Emotional Toxins and the Kidneys:

Metaphysical View: The kidneys, responsible for filtering waste and balancing fluids in the body, are also metaphysically tied to the concept of emotional cleansing. When we refuse to let go of emotional toxins such as guilt, shame, and past trauma, these emotions accumulate and begin to physically impact the kidneys.

Physical Impact: Chronic emotional toxicity that isn't addressed can lead to kidney problems such as chronic kidney disease, kidney infections, or even kidney failure. In metaphysical terms, the kidneys hold onto emotional waste, so the body's physical state is a reflection of unprocessed emotional burdens.

Emotional Reasoning: Emotional toxins— such as unresolved feelings, guilt, fear, or trauma—accumulate in the body when they are not let go out from the heart and body. This is reflected in kidney dysfunction, which serves as a signal to cleanse and release those long-held emotions.

6. Fear and the Bladder:

Metaphysical View: The bladder is often connected to the release of fear and control. Fear of the unknown or fear of losing control can manifest in issues with the bladder, such as incontinence, urinary tract infections, or bladder infections.

Physical Impact: When you hold onto unresolved fears—especially fear of failure, fear of not being good enough, or fear of rejection—it can lead to issues with the bladder, often manifesting as pain or discomfort. Fear is tied to a sense of vulnerability, and when that vulnerability is suppressed, the body creates physical symptoms to release the pent-up emotion.

Emotional Reasoning: When we are unable to release fear and tension, it is physically felt in the bladder, signaling that it is time to let go of control and trust the process of life.

And that's why listen to your emotions and body, body's wisdom and intelligence.

Practices to Tune into the Body

Our emotions can act as powerful signals from our body, warning us of areas in need of healing. When we embrace emotional healing practices like EFT, mindfulness, or even forgiveness, we support the body's ability to heal and restore balance. The organs reflect not just physical health but emotional and energetic states, helping us understand that emotional release is not just an act of mental or spiritual growth—it's a deeply necessary part of maintaining physical well-being.

Each organ has its metaphysical story to tell, urging us to look beyond the surface and listen to the emotional patterns that shape our lives. By healing the emotional body, we can prevent disease, alleviate pain, and achieve a state of holistic wellness.

Here is a powerful practice- body scan, to help you tune into your body, decode its messages, and enhance the connection between your heart and body:

Body Scans: Checking In with Yourself

A body scan is a simple yet profound practice that helps you connect with your physical body and become more aware of any sensations or discomfort. It's a way to listen to the body and discover where emotional blockages or tension might be hiding.

How to Do a Body Scan:

Find a Quiet Space: Sit or lie down in a comfortable position. Close your eyes and take a few deep breaths, inhaling deeply through your nose and exhaling through your mouth.

Start at the Top of Your Head: Bring your awareness to the top of your head. Notice any sensations—whether it's warmth, tightness, or coolness.

Slowly Move Down Your Body: Gently scan your body from head to toe, paying attention to any areas of tension, pain, or discomfort. Observe without judgment or trying to change anything.

Connect to the Feeling: If you find a place of discomfort or tension, breathe into it. Ask yourself, "What emotion or thought might be connected to this feeling?"

Release and Relax: Once you've scanned your body, take a few deep breaths, imagining the tension melting away with each exhale.

This practice can help you uncover where your heart might be holding on to unresolved emotions, stress, or trauma.

The Body's Wisdom

Listening to the body is a skill that requires patience, practice, and self-compassion. Your body is constantly speaking to you — it's a matter of slowing down enough to hear its whispers. The more you practice tuning in, the clearer the messages will become.

When you learn to listen to your body, you strengthen the connection between your heart and your physical self. You begin to trust your intuition and become more aware of how emotions manifest in your body.

So, the next time you feel a physical sensation—whether it's a pain, a twinge, or a sense of lightness—pause and ask yourself: What is my heart trying to communicate through this?

By tuning into your body, you open the door to healing, clarity, and a deeper understanding of yourself.

Chapter 5

Truth 5: The Heart is Connected to Your Intuition and Creativity – Your Heart Knows More Than You Think!

Have you ever had that gut feeling, that inner knowing, when something just feels right—or wrong—without any logical explanation? That's your heart and intuition working together, sending you messages that bypass the mind's need for validation and reasoning. In this chapter, we're going to dive into the profound connection between the heart, intuition, and creativity.

The heart is often seen as the seat of emotion, but did you know it's also a powerful center for intuition and creativity? Your heart has a wisdom that surpasses the limitations of the mind, and when you tune in to it, you open yourself up to a world of deeper insight and inspiration.

Let's explore how this connection works and how you can cultivate it in your life!

Intuition as Heart Intelligence

Intuition is more than just a random feeling or instinct; it's your heart's way of guiding you, even when your mind is uncertain. We've all had moments where we've experienced an intuitive "nudge" to take a certain action or avoid a particular situation. That feeling isn't coming from logic or reasoning—it's coming from the heart's deep intelligence.

Intuition is often described as the "sixth sense," but in truth, it's not a mystical or magical phenomenon. It's a natural function of the heart, where wisdom and guidance arise from an unspoken knowing within us. This knowing comes through as feelings, images, or flashes of insight that arise when we're open to receiving it.

Here's how it works: When the heart is in tune with its wisdom, it becomes a clear channel for intuitive guidance. This is when you start to feel your way through life rather than thinking your way through it. The heart can pick up on subtle energy frequencies in the world around you, guiding you toward decisions, people, and situations that resonate with your higher purpose.

How to Cultivate Your Intuitive Connection to the Heart

We live in a world that often values logic, reasoning, and analysis, which can sometimes block the flow of intuition. The mind can be a powerful tool, but it also loves to overthink and question everything. When you're over-relying on your mind, you may miss out on the wisdom your heart is trying to share. So how do you get back in touch with the heart's intuitive guidance?

Here are a few ways to reconnect with the heart's wisdom:

1. Practice Mindfulness and Presence

The heart speaks in stillness, in moments of quiet. To hear it, you need to be present in the moment. The more present you are in your body and surroundings, the more you can attune yourself to the subtle messages of your heart.

How to Practice:
Take a Pause: Throughout your day, take

short breaks to just breathe and tune into your body. Place a hand on your heart and breathe deeply.

Notice the Body's Sensations: Pay attention to how your body feels in different situations. Does it feel light and expansive or heavy and constricted? Your heart is often sending these physical cues to guide you.

By practicing mindfulness, you create space for intuition to flow freely, allowing you to trust the inner nudges that come from your heart.

2. Trust Your Gut Feelings

We've all heard the saying, "Trust your gut." But what if your gut is your heart's way of speaking to you? Your gut feelings, often referred to as your "first instincts," are deeply connected to your heart and intuition. The more you trust and act on these feelings, the more you'll strengthen your intuitive connection.

How to Develop This Trust:
Start Small: Practice listening to your

intuition in small, low-stakes situations. It could be as simple as trusting the feeling that you should go for a walk or change your route to work.

Notice Patterns: As you trust your gut and act on it, take note of how things unfold. Did your intuition guide you in the right direction? The more you reinforce this process, the stronger your heart's intuitive guidance will become.

3. Let Go of Doubt and Fear

Fear and doubt are the biggest blocks to intuition. When we're caught in self-doubt, we start second-guessing our gut feelings and heart's whispers, often leading us to miss out on valuable insights.

To tap into your heart's wisdom, it's essential to release fear and trust that your heart knows what's best for you. This doesn't mean you'll always have a clear roadmap; it means trusting that your heart will guide you toward the next step, even if the full path isn't visible yet.

The Heart's Role in Creativity

Creativity is another area where the heart's intelligence plays a crucial role. Whether you're an artist, a writer, a businessperson, or someone who simply wants to live a more inspired life, your heart is the wellspring of creative energy.

When we are connected to our hearts, we're more in tune with our authentic selves, and this is where true creativity flows. The heart holds the ability to create without fear—it's the pure expression of our soul's desires and dreams. Creativity, at its core, is about expression, and the heart is the center of that expression.

How to Activate Creative Flow from the Heart

Permit yourself to Create Without Judgment: The heart loves uninhibited self-expression. Allow yourself to create freely, without worrying about whether the outcome is "good enough." When you silence the inner critic, you open the door to unlimited creative potential.

Engage in Creative Play: The heart thrives in playful, joyful environments. Try activities that make you feel alive, whether it's painting, dancing, writing, or simply playing an instrument. These activities allow your heart to speak through creativity.

Tune into Your Emotional Landscape: Your emotions are a rich source of inspiration. Pay attention to what moves you — what excites you, brings you joy, or even makes you feel deeply sad. These emotions are keys to unlocking new creative expressions and ideas.

The Heart's Wisdom in Decision Making

Intuition plays a significant role in how we make decisions. When your heart is open and tuned into its wisdom, it will guide you to the choices that align with your higher purpose.

You know that feeling when you just know something is right for you — when it feels like the most natural decision? That's your heart guiding you. The more you trust your heart's guidance, the more you'll find yourself living in alignment with your true path.

Conclusion: Your Heart Knows More Than You Think

Your heart is a powerful source of intuition and creativity. By learning to listen to its wisdom, you open the door to deeper self-awareness, inspired creativity, and decisions that align with your true purpose. The more you tune into your heart, the more you'll realize that it already holds the answers to many of life's big questions.

So, the next time you find yourself facing a decision, or you need inspiration, ask yourself, what is my heart telling me? Trust in its wisdom, and you'll discover that your heart truly knows more than you think.

Igniting Creativity: Exercises to Strengthen Your Connection to the Heart's Intuitive Wisdom

Creativity is an expression of the heart—it's your soul's language, a beautiful reflection of your innermost desires, dreams, and emotions. When you engage in creative expression, you strengthen your connection to your heart's intuitive wisdom, allowing your heart's guidance to flow more freely into your life. Whether it's through art, writing, or music, creativity helps you listen to and communicate with your heart in profound ways.

Here are some exercises that can help you ignite your creativity and tap into the intuitive wisdom of your heart:

1. Heart-Centered Journaling

Writing is a powerful tool to connect with your heart's deepest thoughts and emotions. Through journaling, you can express the unspoken feelings, beliefs, and ideas that reside in your heart. This exercise allows you to clear mental clutter, tap into your inner wisdom, and uncover hidden truths.

How to Do It:

Set the Scene: Find a quiet space where you can be alone with your thoughts. Light a candle, put on some calming music, or simply sit in silence—whatever feels right to you.

Ask Your Heart a Question: Begin by writing down a question you have or an area of your life where you feel uncertain. It could be your life, career, health, money, work, or even about a decision, a creative project, or a life direction.

Write Freely: Without judgment, allow your pen to flow. Write whatever comes to mind, even if it seems random or disconnected. Don't worry about grammar or structure— just let the words pour out of you.

Reflect on Your Writing: After writing for about 10-15 minutes, take a moment to reread what you've written. Notice any insights, patterns, or feelings that arise. Your heart's wisdom may reveal itself through this practice.

2. Heartful Art Creation

Art is a direct, visual representation of the heart's inner world. Whether you consider yourself an artist or not, creating art can help you express emotions and ideas that are hard to put into words. When you create art from the heart, you tap into a deeper part of yourself that often remains hidden in everyday life.

How to Do It:

Creative Expression Exercise: Unleashing Your Heart's Wisdom

Gather Materials:

Choose your preferred medium—whether it's drawing, painting, collage, digital art, mandala drawing, or pottery.

Mandala Drawing: You can use a compass to create circular patterns or simply draw free-form. The process of creating mandalas has a calming effect and can represent the balance of your inner world.

Pottery: If you prefer working with clay, this can be a deeply tactile, grounding experience. Pottery allows you to mold your emotions into form. Use your hands to shape the clay, paying attention to the texture and how it feels under your touch.

Don't worry about technical skills—this exercise is about expressing your feelings and intuition, so allow yourself to freely explore.

Set an Intention:

Before you begin, take a moment to set an intention for your creative process.

What emotion, thought, or vision do you wish to explore and express through your art? It could be something you want to release, a message you want to uncover, or simply a way to let go of stress or tension.

You may want to focus on healing, clarity, or a specific challenge in your life. The intention helps direct the flow of energy, but remain open to where the process takes you.

Create Freely:

Allow your creativity to flow without any self-imposed rules or restrictions.

Whether you're painting, drawing a mandala, or shaping pottery, allow the process to be led by your emotions and intuition rather than logic or perfectionism.

With mandala drawing, start from the center and work your way out, symbolizing balance and wholeness. With pottery, allow the clay to mold into whatever shape feels right at the moment. Embrace imperfections—they are a part of your expression.

The process is meant to be organic and heartfelt. Let go of any expectations and just *be* in the moment with your creation.

Reflect on the Art:

After finishing your piece, step back and reflect on it.

How does the artwork make you feel? What emotions or thoughts come up when you view it? Does it evoke a sense of peace, release, or joy?

With mandalas, you might notice that the symmetrical patterns bring a sense of harmony or alignment. Pottery may evoke feelings of being grounded, raw, earthy nature of your creativity.

Take time to understand the subtle messages your heart is trying to convey through your art. Is there a hidden theme or symbolism that emerges from the shapes, colors, or textures?

Connect with Your Heart's Wisdom:

Sit in a quiet space after you've completed your creation and connect with your heart.

Ask yourself: *What is my heart trying to tell me through this artwork? What emotions or insights am I uncovering?*

Allow this self-expression to guide you toward clarity, healing, and deeper self-awareness.

Why This Works:

This exercise helps tap into your creative energy, which is deeply connected to your emotions and intuition. Mandalas and pottery are particularly effective in grounding you in the present moment while allowing your inner wisdom to emerge. By embracing art as a tool for self-expression, you align with your heart's true desires and release any emotional blockages.

Remember, it's not about creating a "perfect" piece of art—it's about the experience of creation itself, allowing you to connect more deeply with your inner self.

Whether it's drawing, painting, mandalas, or pottery, each medium has its unique way of channeling energy and facilitating healing.

3. Music and Sound as Heart Connection

Music is a universal language that can deeply connect us to our emotions, intuitions, and the wisdom of our hearts. Whether you play an instrument, sing, or simply listen, music can open the heart and unlock creativity. Engaging with music helps you listen to the heart's rhythmic wisdom.

How to Do It:

Create or Listen to Music: If you play an instrument, try creating music that feels spontaneous and uninhibited. If you don't play an instrument, listen to music that resonates deeply with you. Let the melody and rhythm guide your emotions and intuition.

Tune Into the Sound: As you play or listen, pay attention to how the music makes you feel. Notice any physical sensations or emotions that arise. Allow yourself to be fully immersed in the sound, letting it open up a channel to your heart.

Sing from the Heart: If you sing, try singing with an open heart. Allow your voice to carry your emotions, expressing your inner feelings through sound. You don't need to be perfect—just focus on the connection between your heart and the music.

Don't be amazed, I have learned Tibetan singing bowl sound healing, and I know how I connect with the silent space and just being there, I have even balanced certain chakras and uneasiness.

4. Free-Flow Writing or Automatic Writing

Automatic writing is a practice where you write without consciously thinking, allowing your subconscious mind and heart to guide the words. This exercise helps you access the deeper wisdom that your heart holds, offering insight and clarity on various aspects of your life.

How to Do It:

Set the Scene: Choose a peaceful, quiet environment where you can focus without distractions. Place a pen and paper in front of you and take a few deep breaths.

Ask Your Heart a Question: Before starting, ask your heart a question that is on your mind. It could be something about your current life situation, a creative project, or a decision you need to make.

Let Go and Write: Close your eyes, take a deep breath, and begin writing without stopping. Don't worry about spelling, punctuation, or even making sense—just let the words flow freely. Your hand may move without you thinking, and that's exactly what you want. Trust the process.

Review and Reflect: After writing for 10-15 minutes, read through what you've written. Are there any messages, symbols, or insights that stand out to you? This could be your heart communicating with you through the flow of words.

5. Body Movement and Dance

Movement is a powerful way to unlock your heart's creative energy. When you move your body freely, you connect to the emotional flow within, allowing the heart to guide you. Dance, yoga, and even simple stretching can help release pent-up emotions and stimulate creativity.

How to Do It:

Free Movement: Put on some music that resonates with your emotions, and begin moving your body however it feels. Don't worry about form or structure—just let your body express itself freely.

Embody the Emotion: As you move, focus on the emotions you're feeling. Let your body express what words can't, whether it's joy, frustration, love, or sadness.

Practice Yoga or Qi Gong: These practices combine movement, breath, and mindfulness to activate the heart's energy and release emotional blockages. Whether it's through flowy movements or slow, mindful poses, these practices help you tap into your heart's creative energy.

6. Creating a Heart-Centered Vision Board

A vision board is a visual representation of your dreams, goals, and intentions. It helps you connect with your heart's desires and align your actions with your true purpose. By gathering images, words, and symbols that resonate with your heart, you create a powerful visual reminder of your soul's intentions.

How to Do It:

Gather Supplies: Collect magazines, newspapers, or printouts of images and words that resonate with your heart's desires. You'll also need scissors, glue, and a large board or poster.

Visualize Your Heart's Desires: Before you start, take a few moments to connect with your heart. Close your eyes, breathe deeply, and ask your heart what it truly wants to create or manifest in your life.

Create Your Vision Board: Cut out images and words that align with your heart's desires and glue them onto your board. Don't worry about making it perfect—just follow the intuitive guidance of your heart.

Display Your Vision Board: Place the vision board somewhere you can see it daily. Let it be a constant reminder of the dreams and creative energy that are waiting to flow through your heart.

Conclusion: Creativity as a Gateway to the Heart

Through these exercises, you've begun to awaken the creative flow that resides within your heart. Whether you engage in art, writing, music, or movement, each form of creative expression brings you closer to the intuitive wisdom your heart holds. The more you practice these exercises, the stronger your connection to your heart's creative energy will become, and the more easily your heart's wisdom will flow into all areas of your life.

So, what will you create today?

My personal story of intuition and creativity

I wasn't always intuitive. It wasn't something that came naturally to me. But over time, I've learned to tap into it, and today, intuition is one of my most trusted companions. It's fascinating how Tarot cards have played such a pivotal role in this journey. When I first started learning Tarot, I wasn't entirely sure how everything would come together. But there was something about those cards—about the pictures and symbols—that spoke to me in ways words could not.

Through my connection with the cards, I started finding clarity amidst my confusion and uncertainties. You know how life can feel like a series of jumbled thoughts, and sometimes, it's difficult to see beyond the fog of doubt? The cards offered me that clarity. They helped me find guidance when I was unsure, opening doors of insight I never knew existed.

I began to understand how the Major Arcana guides the significant phases of life, the milestones, the turning points—those big, transformative events that shape us. The Four Minor Arcana suits, with their unique qualities, helped me make sense of the smaller, everyday aspects of life: thinking, feeling, sensing, and acting. As I connected with these cards, I discovered that the true art of Tarot isn't just about interpreting the symbols—it's about linking the head and heart, the mind and body, the heart and soul.

Isn't it interesting how we all go through life with different kinds of struggles and questions? We're all trying to make sense of our paths, wondering if we're on the right one, asking ourselves if there's something more we could do to move forward. I realized that Tarot had the power to bring people new perspectives. It wasn't just about reading the cards—it was about helping others see things they couldn't see before, helping them step back, shift their focus, and view their challenges from a fresh angle.

In my work as a Tarot coach, I've had the privilege of guiding over 17,000 people— each with their unique concerns, questions, and issues. Every reading I've done has opened my eyes to a new layer of human experience. The beauty of Tarot is that it allows us to dive deep into those layers, uncovering hidden truths, resolving old patterns, and releasing blocks. Through Tarot, I've been able to provide guidance that isn't just about predicting the future—it's about helping people understand the patterns of their past, empowering them to make better choices, and equipping them with the tools they need to create positive change in their lives.

It's so inspiring to see how the Tarot cards, combined with my other healing and coaching knowledge, have shaped my ability to create real, lasting change. The integration of all these aspects of life—healing, coaching, counseling—has truly made me who I am today as a Tarot coach. It's a beautiful blend of intuition, knowledge, and creativity that helps me serve others in meaningful ways.

But here's the thing: You don't have to be born with intuition to develop it. You don't have to be naturally gifted with psychic abilities to connect with the cards. It's all about practice, trust, and listening to that quiet, inner voice. When you begin to tune in to your intuitive wisdom, you realize how much guidance is already available to you—through the cards, through your heart, and your soul.

And here's the interesting part: Besides intuition, Tarot has unlocked my creativity too. It's inspired me to invent my own Empowerment Oracle cards and even start authoring books, soon you will find them in the market! My very first book, My Creativity was written in 15 days, self-published, and marketed without much editing, and it was a completely divine channeled book, "The Inner Journey" an example of free-flow writing.   My cards and books are not just tools; they are pieces of my soul, born from my journey, my struggles, and my achievements. Each word comes straight from the heart, reflecting the lessons I've learned along the way. Soon, these creations will reach millions, sharing the wisdom and healing I've gained with others. It's incredible to think that what once began as my own story is now ready to inspire and guide so many. The Universe has aligned, and the ripple effect of healing and transformation has begun. Are you there on the healing path with me?

Who would have thought that a journey that began with questions and curiosity would lead me to a space where I can create tools that inspire others to walk their paths with confidence? Thank you, Universe, for guiding me to this place where everything aligns so beautifully.

Nowadays, people have started following their heart, soul, and passion. Their choices are solely depending on their passion. Have you ever felt that spark of curiosity or that nudge in your heart to explore something new, to trust in a process, or to unlock a hidden talent? That's your intuition calling. It's there, waiting for you to recognize it. Tarot, for me, has been the tool to enhance my intuition and creativity, also a guiding pathway to self-discovery and transformation. For me, my calling was Tarot, healing, and coaching, and I followed and flowed with it. How might your life shift if you listened to that inner voice?

What doors might open for you if you trust in your wisdom?

As I continue this journey of learning, teaching, and creating, I feel incredibly grateful for everything that has come my way. I know that Tarot, intuition, and creativity are not just gifts—they're tools that can transform lives. As a coach, my mission is to help others connect with their power, discover their insights, and step into a future that feels aligned with their true selves.

So, what's calling you? What's waiting for you on the other side of your intuition?

Have you noticed how many questions have been raised in this book? There's a purpose behind that. You see, I believe that questions hold the power to unlock infinite knowledge. The universe is vast and filled with endless possibilities, and each question we ask is like a key that opens a new door to understanding.

The beauty of asking questions is that it encourages us to expands our minds. It encourages us to think beyond the limitations we set for ourselves and opens us up to new perspectives and deeper insights. The answers we seek may be multiple, and that's what makes the journey so exciting. When we ask, we invite creativity, intuition, and the flow of possibilities into our lives.

Think about it: if we only chose one answer for each question, we would be limiting ourselves. But by simply asking, we create space for infinite answers to unfold. And in that space, our awareness grows, and so does our capacity to connect with the wisdom around us.

Asking questions is a way to transcend our limitations, explore beyond what we know, and allow our creativity and intuition to lead the way. So, the next time you find yourself with a question, remember that it's not just a search for one answer; it's an invitation to discover countless possibilities.

Here are some questions that can help you unlock deeper insights into your intuition and creativity, clearing the way for more expansive thinking and allowing you to step into your full creative potential, would you give some time to yourself, pause, use your notes, and pen or digital notes, whatever suits you to answer them.

Here are some questions designed to ignite your intuition and creativity:

What if the answers you've been seeking are already within you? What if your intuition is the most reliable guide you have?

What would it take for you to trust your creative impulses completely and act on them without hesitation?

What if you were willing to let go of all the judgments, doubts, and limitations that block your creative flow?

How much more creative could you be if you stopped asking for permission and started listening to the whispers of your heart?

What if intuition isn't something to figure out, but something to follow? What if your gut feeling is your highest truth guiding you forward?

What possibilities could unfold if you allowed yourself to create without worrying about what others think?

What if there is no "right" or "wrong" in your creative process—only your unique expression unfolding?

How much space can you create for your intuition to show up, and what could be possible if you trusted it fully?

If you acknowledged the creative power within you, what would you choose to create right now?

What would happen if you stopped thinking and allowed your creativity to flow from a place of pure being, without any expectations or limitations?

Enjoy connecting with your intuitive and creative powers!

Enjoy asking questions and getting some insights too!

Enjoy you discovering your true self!

Enjoy being a possibiltarian to tap into infinite powers!

Chapter 6

Truth 6: The Heart's Intelligence Can Heal You – It Holds Infinite Wisdom

Healing Power of the Heart

Did you know that your heart has a natural ability to heal you—emotionally, physically, and spiritually? While we often look to external solutions, medications, or therapies to heal ourselves, the true power to heal lies within us, in the infinite wisdom of our hearts.

The heart is more than just a vital organ—it is a profound source of intelligence, a guiding force that can lead you to healing, clarity, and peace. It is the seat of your emotions, your intuition, and your deepest desires, and it holds the key to transforming challenges into opportunities for growth and self-discovery.

The Heart's Role in Emotional Healing

Every wound you've experienced, whether physical or emotional, has left an imprint on your heart. Whether it's the loss of a loved one, a traumatic event, or years of emotional neglect, these experiences create imbalances in your energy and emotional body. But the heart is capable of processing these wounds and turning them into profound wisdom.

When you begin to listen to your heart, you start to unlock its healing power. The heart has a deep connection to your emotions and the ability to release and transform them. It doesn't just store pain—it knows how to release it, transform it, and guide you through the process of healing.

Think about this: Have you ever had a moment where you felt an overwhelming sense of love, kindness, or compassion for yourself or someone else? That feeling came from your heart, and it was healing. When you align with your heart's energy, you create space for healing and transformation.

The Heart's Healing Energy and Health

Your physical body and your heart are deeply connected, more than you might realize. It's said that the heart doesn't just pump blood—it also pumps emotional energy, which circulates throughout the body, affecting your health and well-being.

When your heart is in a state of emotional imbalance, that energy is disrupted, and physical ailments can arise. We have read in previous truths, that stress, anger, grief, and anxiety can manifest as physical pain, chronic illness, or fatigue. But here's the incredible part: When you reconnect with your heart, you can heal those emotional wounds and, in turn, your physical body.

It's been scientifically shown that practicing heart-centered activities like meditation, deep breathing, and gratitude can reduce stress and boost your immune system. The heart has the unique ability to influence your body's energy field, promoting balance, healing, and overall well-being.

Spiritual Healing Through the Heart

On a spiritual level, the heart holds the key to your soul's journey. It is the bridge between your physical self and your higher consciousness. Your heart is not only your emotional center but also the seat of your spiritual wisdom.

When you open your heart to its infinite wisdom, you begin to reconnect with your true essence. You'll find that you no longer feel disconnected or lost, but rather, deeply aligned with your purpose. You gain clarity on what truly matters, and you start living in harmony with your soul's calling.

Practical Ways to Tap into the Heart's Healing Power

Now that you understand the incredible healing power of your heart, how can you tap into it more consciously? Here are some practical tools you can use to connect with your heart's infinite wisdom:

1. Heart-Centered Meditation

Meditation is one of the most powerful tools for connecting with your heart's intelligence. By focusing your attention on your heart center, you can bring healing energy to your emotional, physical, and spiritual bodies.

How to Do It:

Find a quiet space where you can sit comfortably.

Close your eyes and take a few deep breaths, allowing your body to relax.

Place your hands over your heart and feel the warmth of your palms on your chest.

Visualize a bright, healing light glowing in the center of your heart.

Focus on your breath and the energy in your heart, allowing it to expand with each inhale and release any tension with each exhale.

Stay in this space for 10-15 minutes, allowing your heart to guide you to peace and healing.

2. Heartful Affirmations

Your heart responds powerfully to positive, loving affirmations. Repeating heart-centered affirmations helps reprogram your mind and energy, allowing your heart's healing wisdom to flow freely.

Examples of Heartful Affirmations:

"I am worthy of love, health, and happiness."

"My heart is a source of infinite wisdom and healing."

"I release all past pain and open my heart to healing and love."

"I trust in the healing power of my heart and body."

"I am connected to the infinite wisdom within me."

Repeat these affirmations daily, especially when you feel disconnected or overwhelmed. Feel the words resonating in your heart as you say them.

3. Breathing Into the Heart

Breath is one of the most powerful tools for bringing balance and healing to your heart. When you consciously breathe into your heart space, you activate its natural ability to heal and release tension.

How to Do It:

Sit in a comfortable position and take a few deep breaths.

Place one hand over your heart and the other on your abdomen.

With each inhale, imagine breathing in healing energy into your heart.

As you exhale, visualize releasing any tension, fear, or pain from your heart.

Continue this breathing pattern for 5-10 minutes, allowing the healing energy to fill your heart and body.

4. Acts of Self-Love

One of the most important ways to activate your heart's healing power is through self-love. The heart responds deeply to acts of kindness and care, and when you show love to yourself, you create a healing environment within your own heart.

Ways to Practice Self-Love:

Take time each day to do something that nourishes you—whether it's reading a book, taking a walk, or practicing a hobby you love.

Speak kindly to yourself, and avoid negative self-talk.

Honor your body by nourishing it with healthy food, exercise, and rest.

Set boundaries that honor your needs and protect your energy.

5. Gratitude Practice

Gratitude is a powerful healing tool that directly impacts the heart. When you express gratitude, you open your heart to receiving more love, abundance, and healing energy. Gratitude shifts your focus from what's lacking to what is abundant in your life, allowing your heart to vibrate at a higher frequency.

How to Do It:

Every morning or evening, write down 3 things you are grateful for. They don't have to be big; even small moments of joy can have a profound effect.

As you reflect on each blessing, take a moment to feel deep gratitude in your heart. Allow that feeling of thankfulness to fill you up, healing any pain or heaviness.

Conclusion: Trusting Your Heart's Healing Power

Your heart is an incredibly powerful source of healing, wisdom, and guidance. When you listen to its whispers and trust its intelligence, you begin to unlock your body's innate ability to heal, grow, and evolve. Whether it's emotional pain, physical illness, or spiritual disconnection, your heart holds the key to overcoming it all.

By consciously connecting with your heart through practices like meditation, affirmations, breathwork, self-love, and gratitude, you activate its healing energy, transforming your life from the inside out.

So, what if the healing you've been searching for is already within you, waiting to be unlocked by your heart's infinite wisdom?

How to Connect with Your Heart's Wisdom:

Connecting with your heart's wisdom is a transformative process that allows you to tap into your deepest truth, intuition, and inner guidance. It's about moving beyond the noise of daily life and tuning into the gentle whispers of your heart. Often, we get so caught up in our heads, analyzing, thinking, and worrying about the future or the past. But true clarity and wisdom reside in the heart, and it has the answers that our minds may overlook.

Pause and Breathe: The first step to connecting with your heart's wisdom is to quiet the mind. In our busy world, we are constantly bombarded with thoughts and distractions. To hear your heart, you need to create a space of stillness. Simply sit in a quiet space, close your eyes, and take a few deep breaths. Allow your body to relax with each exhale. Let go of the tension, and let your body feel light and grounded.

Focus on Your Heart: Place your hand gently on your chest, over your heart. Tune into the rhythmic beats of your heart. With each beat, feel a connection to the energy that flows through you. You can even visualize a warm, golden light radiating from your heart, symbolizing the wisdom and love that resides within. This simple act helps to bring your awareness to your heart space.

Ask the Right Questions: Once you're grounded in your heart, ask yourself questions that reflect your inner desires or concerns. The key is to ask open-ended questions that allow the heart to guide you, such as:

"What does my heart truly desire?"

"What path will bring me the most peace?"

"What do I need to let go of to live authentically?" By asking these types of questions, you open the door for your heart to respond.

Trust the Feelings and Insights You Receive: When you connect with your heart, you may receive intuitive thoughts, images, or feelings. Trust whatever arises, even if it doesn't always make sense. Your heart's wisdom isn't always logical or linear—it's deeply rooted in your emotions and soul's knowing. Pay attention to the subtle sensations, such as a deep sense of peace, excitement, or clarity.

Let Your Heart Speak: Sometimes, the wisdom of the heart is not verbal, but rather a feeling of inner knowing. Don't force anything—allow the wisdom to come naturally. Let your heart speak through feelings, dreams, or even signs that may appear in your day-to-day life. Be open and receptive.

Guided Meditation: Connecting with Your Heart's Wisdom

Here is a simple guided meditation to help you connect with your heart's wisdom.

Find a Comfortable Position: Sit in a comfortable chair or lie down with your hands resting on your lap or by your sides. Close your eyes, and begin to take slow, deep breaths. Inhale deeply through your nose, and exhale through your mouth. With each breath, allow your body to relax further.

Relax and Center Yourself: Imagine a warm golden light glowing softly around you. With each breath, feel this light growing stronger and surrounding your entire body. Let it bring you a sense of calm, peace, and comfort. Let go of any tension in your muscles, face, or neck. Feel your body becoming grounded and balanced.

Focus on Your Heart: Now, place your hand gently over your chest, right over your heart. Feel the steady beat of your heart under your palm. With every heartbeat, imagine a warm, golden light expanding from your heart, filling your chest with warmth, love, and wisdom. This light represents the wisdom of your heart.

Ask Your Heart a Question: Quietly ask your heart a question that's been on your mind. It could be related to your life purpose, your relationships, or your personal growth. You might ask, "What do I need to know right now?" or "What is the next step for me?"

Be Open to the Answer: As you breathe, simply allow yourself to be open and receptive. You may not receive an immediate answer, and that's okay. Trust that the wisdom will come when you are ready. It may come as a word, a picture, or even a subtle shift in how you feel.

Affirm Your Heart's Wisdom: As you sit in this space of stillness, affirm to yourself, "I trust my heart's wisdom. I trust my inner guidance. I am open to receiving the messages my heart is sending me."

Sit in Silence: Spend a few more minutes sitting in silence, absorbing the energy of your heart's wisdom. Allow the messages, feelings, or clarity to come through naturally. Trust whatever arises. Know that your heart always holds the answers you seek.

Bring the Meditation to a Close: Slowly bring your awareness back to your body and the present moment. Wiggle your fingers and toes, and take a few deep breaths. When you feel ready, gently open your eyes. Feel a sense of gratitude for the connection you've just made with your heart's wisdom.

Heart-Centered Breathing Alignment Process

All you need is your alignment with your heart! The Heart-Centered Breathing Alignment process helps you tune into your heart space, bringing your body and mind into alignment with your highest self. This technique encourages relaxation, emotional balance, and clarity, as well as a deeper connection to your intuition. By focusing on your heart and breath, you can create a harmonious flow of energy throughout your body, fostering peace and clarity.

Steps for Heart-Centered Breathing Alignment:

Find a Comfortable Position:

Sit or lie down in a comfortable position. You can sit cross-legged on the floor or in a chair with your feet flat on the ground.

Rest your hands gently on your lap or knees, and keep your spine straight, and shoulders relaxed.

Close Your Eyes:

Gently close your eyes to eliminate external distractions and focus your attention inward.

Focus on Your Breath:

Take a few deep breaths in through your nose, allowing your belly to expand fully as you inhale, and gently releasing the breath through your mouth, letting go of any tension or stress.

Continue breathing deeply, but now begin to focus on your heart. Imagine your breath coming in and out through your heart center, just in the middle of your chest.

Engage the Heart:

As you breathe, gently place your hand over your heart. Feel the warmth of your hand and connect with the natural rhythm of your heartbeat.

With each breath, inhale deeply into your heart, allowing the energy to expand, and exhale through your heart, releasing any negative emotions or tension.

Activate Heart-Centered Energy:

Imagine a soft, warm light glowing in the center of your chest, radiating out from your heart. Visualize this light growing brighter with every breath.

As you breathe in, visualize this light expanding, filling your entire chest cavity. As you exhale, see the light flowing out through your body, filling every part of you with peace and love.

With each breath, feel your heart center becoming more open and aligned with your highest truth.

Balance Your Mind and Heart:

As you continue to breathe, gently ask your heart what it wants you to know. Trust whatever comes to you, whether it's a feeling, a thought, or an image.

If your mind starts to wander or you begin to feel any resistance, gently guide your attention back to your heart. Focus on your breath and the warmth of the light in your heart.

Allow your mind to quiet as you stay anchored in the heart's wisdom and energy. This helps align the head and heart, creating a balanced state of mind and emotions.

Use a Heart-Centered Affirmation:

As you breathe, you can repeat a heart-centered affirmation, such as:

"I am connected to the wisdom of my heart."

"My heart guides me with love and clarity."

"I trust the wisdom and flow of my heart."

Let these words flow through you with each breath, anchoring the alignment between your heart and mind.

Sit in Stillness:

Continue breathing deeply for a few more minutes, allowing yourself to stay present with your heart's wisdom and the gentle rhythm of your breath.

Experience the peace, alignment, and clarity that comes from connecting deeply with your heart center.

Gradually Return to the Present Moment:

When you're ready to complete the practice, slowly begin to bring your awareness back to your body. Gently wiggle your fingers and toes, and take a few grounding breaths.

Feel your body relaxed, centered, and aligned with your heart. Open your eyes slowly when you're ready, carrying the peace and alignment of your heart with you throughout your day.

Benefits of Heart-Centered Breathing Alignment:

Emotional Balance: Helps release stress and negative emotions, creating space for more peace, love, and compassion.

Mental Clarity: Aligns your thoughts with your inner truth, allowing you to make decisions from a centered and balanced place.

Enhanced Intuition: Strengthens the connection with your inner wisdom, helping you to tune into your intuition and trust the messages your heart offers.

Physical Relaxation: Promotes overall relaxation, helping to release physical tension stored in the body, particularly in the chest, shoulders, and neck.

Inner Peace: Cultivates a sense of deep inner peace and calm, which flows into all areas of your life.

This heart-centered alignment process is a simple yet powerful way to connect to your true self and live more mindfully. It can be practiced daily or whenever you need to realign and center yourself.

Chapter 7

Truth 7: The Heart is the Seat of Consciousness

When we think of consciousness, we often think of the mind—thoughts, logic, reason, and mental clarity. But what if I told you that the true seat of consciousness is not just the brain, but the heart? The heart, often seen as the center of emotion, actually holds a far more profound role in our overall awareness and presence.

The heart is not just a pump for blood—it is a powerful, intelligent center that houses wisdom far beyond our mental understanding. It is the true source of emotional intelligence, spiritual awareness, and higher consciousness. Think about this: When you feel a deep sense of knowing, an intuitive "gut feeling" that seems to come from nowhere, is it truly coming from your mind? Or is it the subtle, yet powerful intelligence of the heart speaking to you?

The Heart's Intelligence
Scientific studies have shown that the heart

has its independent neural network, often referred to as the "heart brain." This neural network allows the heart to process information, make decisions, and even communicate with the brain. It is in constant dialogue with our mind, influencing our emotions, thoughts, and actions.

The heart is constantly receiving and processing energy from our surroundings, and it is deeply connected to the flow of energy in our body. This makes the heart a powerful tool for understanding not only ourselves but the universe around us. It taps into universal intelligence and directs us towards what is most aligned with our true essence.

Connecting to Your Heart's Wisdom

When we focus on connecting with our hearts, we access a space of deep knowing and clarity. It is here that we can receive guidance that transcends the limitations of our logical minds. The heart helps us make decisions that are aligned with our authentic selves, allowing us to navigate life with more ease, grace, and confidence.

But how do we connect with this wisdom? By practicing heart-centered activities such as mindfulness, meditation, and deep breathing, we can open ourselves to the heart's subtle messages. By learning to trust what we feel in our hearts, we can quiet the noise of our overactive minds and tap into a deeper consciousness—one that is in tune with both our highest self and the universe.

Living from the Heart

When we live from the heart, we experience a life of greater flow and harmony. We stop overthinking, stop doubting, and start trusting the intuitive wisdom that comes naturally to us. The heart aligns us with our true purpose and helps us manifest our desires in ways that feel authentic and meaningful.

When we connect to the heart's wisdom, we shift from merely existing to truly living, creating a life that resonates with joy, peace, and fulfillment. This conscious shift in awareness is not just a mental exercise but an embodied experience that transforms our entire being.

The heart, in its simplicity and profound wisdom, holds the keys to our true consciousness. By learning to listen to it and trust its guidance, we can unlock a world of possibilities and step into a life of alignment and purpose.

Heart vs. Head: A Deeper Form of Awareness

The conscious mind is often caught in a loop of thoughts—questions, judgments, reasoning, and plans. It's always moving, always analyzing. But the heart doesn't work this way. The heart is silent, subtle, and deeply connected to a form of awareness that goes beyond rational thought. It operates from a space of pure presence, guiding us not through logic, but through feelings and intuition.

The heart's consciousness isn't chaotic or loud; it's deep and expansive, radiating a quiet, steady pulse of truth. When we are connected to the heart, we move into a state of being present in the moment—what some may call mindfulness. It allows us to be fully alive and aware, not just mentally, but spiritually and emotionally.

This form of consciousness doesn't only deal with our emotional state. It connects us to a broader awareness of our existence, our purpose, and our soul's mission. The heart is the gateway to self-awareness and spiritual insight, leading us toward deeper levels of consciousness.

We are all inherently beings of love and light, and it's through our awareness and consciousness that we can transform, just like charcoal into a diamond. Let me explain this concept from a more aligned perspective:

We are Love and Light Beings

At our core, we are beings of infinite love and light—pure, divine energy. We come into this world with immense potential, but as we grow, we often experience life's challenges, conditioning, and limiting beliefs. These layers cover our innate brilliance, just as coal might be hidden deep within the earth, not yet revealing its true potential.

Awareness is the key to unlocking this hidden light within us. It is the tool that helps us peel away the layers of conditioning, fear, and negativity. It's like shining a light on the dark corners of our minds and hearts, illuminating the path to our true essence.

Charcoal to Diamond: The Transformation of Consciousness

We start as charcoal, representing the raw state of our being, full of potential but perhaps weighed down by life's experiences. As we become more aware—of our thoughts, emotions, actions, and spiritual nature—we begin to transform. This process is not instantaneous, but through consistent effort, mindfulness, self-reflection, and healing, we begin to shed the old, limiting patterns and rise above them.

Think of the charcoal as our challenges, our unresolved emotions, and our fears. These are the things that weigh us down and prevent us from fully shining. But when we bring awareness to them, when we observe and process them with love and compassion, we start to transmute this energy. The more we align with the light of our true nature, the more we begin to shine, just like the diamond.

The Role of Awareness

Awareness is the catalyst for this transformation. It's the light that illuminates our true self. Through awareness, we begin to see ourselves for who we truly are: beings of light, untainted by the external world's limitations. As we raise our consciousness, we move from being a piece of charcoal—raw, untapped potential—to becoming a radiant diamond, a manifestation of our highest truth and purpose.

When we recognize our inherent worth and the infinite love within us, we start to operate from a place of peace, compassion, and joy. Our challenges become stepping stones, and we learn that everything, even our darkest moments, is part of our spiritual evolution. The more we awaken, the more our true light shines through, just like the diamond, radiant and brilliant.

Living as Diamond Beings of Love and Light

Ultimately, through the power of awareness and consciousness, we remember that we are love and light. We are divine beings, capable of transforming any hardship into wisdom, and any challenge into growth. By connecting with our true essence—through mindfulness, healing, and self-awareness—we continuously evolve, becoming more radiant, more loving, and more aligned with our higher selves.

Just like a diamond is a symbol of purity, strength, and clarity, we too can embody these qualities as we walk our journey on Earth, shedding layers that no longer serve us and embracing the light that we are. The more we expand our awareness, the closer we get to realizing that we are already whole, already perfect, and already loved.

Conclusion

You are not just a piece of charcoal—you are the diamond in the making. Through awareness, conscious living, through healing, you uncover the brilliant, radiant being that you have always been. Let your light shine brightly and know that you are always, always love and light.

How the Heart Opens Us to Higher Consciousness

Heart-Centered Awareness:

When we begin to live from the heart, we open ourselves to greater awareness. This isn't just about being aware of our emotions, but also being present with the world around us. The heart knows how to connect us with the flow of life, recognizing patterns that the mind might miss. It speaks to us through emotions and gut feelings, guiding us when logic fails.

Living in Alignment:

When we're aligned with our heart's consciousness, we begin to make decisions based on intuition, rather than overthinking. This allows us to step into flow—a state where life feels less like a struggle and more like a harmonious unfolding. In this state, the heart's intelligence helps us trust the process of life, knowing that each experience is a part of our soul's journey.

Expanded Awareness:
The heart is a powerful energy center that connects us to higher dimensions of consciousness. It is said that the heart can resonate with universal energy, tapping into a collective consciousness that transcends individual experience. When we are connected to the heart, we are connected to the pulse of life itself. We see the interconnectedness of all beings and understand that our actions have ripples far beyond what the mind can grasp.

Affirmations

The Right Way to Affirm – A Stepwise Understanding

Affirmations are powerful tools for transformation, but they work best when practiced mindfully and with intention. Simply repeating words like a parrot won't bring true change. Here's how to affirm effectively:

1. Believe in Your Affirmation

Affirmations are not just words; they are energy. Before saying them, take a moment to feel their truth. If you don't believe in what you're saying, your subconscious may resist the change. If necessary, modify the affirmation to something you can accept.

Example: Instead of "I am completely confident," try "I learn to trust myself more each day."

2. Feel the Emotion Behind It

The power of affirmations lies in the emotions they evoke. When you affirm something, let yourself feel the joy, confidence, peace, or gratitude as if it's already true.

Example: Saying "I am worthy of love" with deep self-compassion creates a much stronger impact than just repeating the words.

3. Use Present Tense, Not Future Tense

Affirmations work in the now. If you say, "I will be successful," it always remains in the future. Instead, affirm the present moment.

 Example: Say, "I am aligned with success" instead of "I will be successful."

4. Be Specific and Clear

Vague affirmations create vague results. The more precise you are, the more powerful the affirmation becomes.

 Example: Instead of "I am happy," try "I wake up every morning feeling grateful, peaceful, and excited for my day."

5. Align Body, Mind, and Breath

Speak your affirmations with full awareness. Breathe deeply before affirming, say the words with conviction, and visualize them as reality. You can also place your hand on your heart or solar plexus for a deeper connection.

Example: If affirming self-love, place your hand on your heart and feel the warmth radiating as you say, "I deeply and completely love and accept myself."

6. Repeat with Consistency, Not Just Repetition

Affirmations are like seeds—you must nurture them daily with belief and action. Saying them once a day and forgetting about them won't bring results. Instead, repeat them with mindfulness throughout the day, especially during moments of self-doubt. Example: If affirming abundance, practice it when making financial decisions or expressing gratitude for what you already have.

7. Take Inspired Action

Affirmations align your energy, but action solidifies them. If you affirm, "I am a confident speaker," take small steps like speaking up in a meeting or practicing your voice in the mirror. Affirmations + action = transformation.

Example: If you are affirming "I attract healthy relationships," then also work on setting boundaries and practicing self-love.

Final Thought

Affirmations are not magic spells; they are tools to rewire your subconscious. When practiced with belief, feeling, and action, they create profound shifts in your reality,

Here are some powerful affirmations using the words I recognize, I realign, and I transform to create a shift in mindfulness, healing, and self-awareness:

I recognize the power within me to heal and release what no longer serves my highest good.

I realign my mind, body, and soul with the flow of positive energy and inner peace.

I transform every challenge into an opportunity for growth, awakening, and self-discovery.

I recognize my worth and embrace my authentic self with love and compassion.

I realign my thoughts to reflect balance, clarity, and a deep sense of inner calm.

I transform my old patterns into new ways of thinking, being, and thriving.

I recognize that every moment is a chance to reconnect with my true essence and wisdom.

I realign my actions to honor my body, mind, and soul, knowing I am worthy of healing.

I transform all emotional blocks into light, allowing myself to fully express my truth and vitality.

I recognize that self-awareness is my greatest tool for living in peace and harmony.

I realign with the present moment, embracing each breath as a reminder of my connection to the universe.

I transform my past pains into wisdom, allowing me to step into my full potential with grace and confidence.

These affirmations, repeated daily, can guide you to realign your energy, recognize your true potential, and transform any aspect of yourself that needs healing and awareness.

Exercise for expanding awareness

Expanding awareness involves tapping into deeper levels of consciousness and understanding beyond the immediate, habitual patterns of the mind. It's about moving from limited thinking to a more expansive and connected state of being. Here are some tools and exercises you can use to create expanded awareness:

1. Mindfulness Meditation

Mindfulness meditation is one of the most effective ways to expand awareness. It helps you become more present and tuned in to your body, mind, and surroundings. Here's how you can practice:

Find a quiet space where you won't be disturbed.

Sit comfortably and focus on your breath.

Bring your attention to each inhale and exhale, noticing the sensations in your body as you breathe.

When your mind wanders, gently guide it back to the breath, acknowledging the thoughts without judgment.

Expand your focus over time to include sensations, sounds, and feelings that arise. This trains you to be present with whatever is happening at the moment.

2. Body Scan Awareness

This exercise enhances awareness by connecting you with the physical sensations in your body, helping you notice areas of tension, discomfort, or relaxation.

Lie down or sit comfortably.

Close your eyes and take a few deep breaths to relax.

Start at your toes and slowly bring your attention upward, one body part at a time.

Notice the sensations in each area—whether it's warmth, tension, or lightness.

Breathe into each area as you move your awareness, allowing it to soften or release tension.

By the end, you'll have a greater connection to your body and an expanded awareness of how your physical state affects your emotions and thoughts.

3. Journaling for Awareness

Writing can be a powerful tool to bring unconscious thoughts and feelings to the surface, allowing you to explore them in depth.

Set aside a few minutes each day to journal.

Ask yourself open-ended questions, such as:

What am I feeling right now?

What is my body telling me?

How am I limiting myself in this moment?

Write freely, without judgment or concern for grammar. Let your thoughts flow.

After journaling, reflect on the patterns that appear in your writing. This helps increase self-awareness and identify limiting beliefs or habitual ways of thinking.

4. Expand Your Perspective Through New Experiences

To break free from old patterns of thinking and expand awareness, it's essential to expose yourself to new ideas, experiences, and environments. Here's how you can do this:

Travel to a new place—whether it's a physical location or exploring a new topic.

Engage in a creative hobby that's outside your usual comfort zone.

Read books, listen to podcasts, or attend lectures that challenge your current beliefs and stretch your mind.

Volunteer or help others—serving others can provide a fresh perspective on life and help you break out of your usual self-focused thoughts.

5. Breathwork and Pranayama

Breathwork is an ancient tool that helps calm the mind and expand consciousness. It enables you to access deeper states of awareness and emotional clarity.

Find a comfortable sitting position, keeping your back straight.

Start by taking deep breaths, focusing on each inhale and exhale.

Try the 4-7-8 breathing technique:

Inhale deeply for 4 counts.

Hold your breath for 7 counts.

Exhale slowly for 8 counts.

Repeat the cycle for several rounds. With practice, this breathing exercise calms the nervous system and helps you connect with deeper layers of your consciousness.

6. Visualization Techniques

Visualization is a powerful tool for expanding awareness. It allows you to see beyond the limitations of the physical world and tap into the wisdom of the mind and spirit.

Sit in a quiet place and close your eyes.

Imagine a place that makes you feel at peace, whether it's real or imagined.

Visualize yourself expanding—see your energy and awareness extending beyond your body, enveloping the environment around you.

Feel your connection to everything—the people, nature, and even the universe itself.

Practice this regularly to open yourself to a higher level of awareness.

7. Self-Inquiry (The Work by Byron Katie)

Self-inquiry is a process of examining your thoughts and beliefs to see if they are true and to expand your awareness of how they affect your life.

Pick a belief or thought that causes stress or discomfort.

Ask yourself four questions:

Is it true?

Can I know if it's true?

How do I react when I believe this thought?

Who would I be without this thought?

Turn the thought around to see if the opposite or a new perspective could be true.

This practice helps you shift limiting beliefs and expand your awareness of how your thoughts create your reality.

8. Gratitude Practice

Gratitude opens the heart and creates a shift in awareness toward abundance and positivity.

Write down three things you're grateful for each day—no matter how small or big they are.

Feel the gratitude deeply in your heart as you write them down.

Reflect on the abundance in your life, even in challenging times.

Gratitude helps you shift your focus from what's lacking to what's already present, expanding your awareness of the richness around you. These techniques help clear blocked energy and create space for expanded awareness. You can do this through self-healing practices or by working with a practitioner.

These techniques help clear blocked energy and create space for expanded awareness. You can do this through self-healing practices or by working with a practitioner.

These techniques help clear blocked energy and create space for expanded awareness. You can do this through self-healing practices or by working with a practitioner.

These techniques help clear blocked energy and create space for expanded awareness. You can do this through self-healing practices or by working with a practitioner.

These techniques help clear blocked energy and create space for expanded awareness. You can do this through self-healing practices or by working with a practitioner.

In Reiki, you channel healing energy through your hands to clear blocked energy in your own or others' bodies.

In Redikall consciousness, you exactly learn how healing and resolution can be achieved by understanding and clearing the mind and energetic blocks. It's must read book by Aatmn, my dear mentor- '*The Redikall Crystalline Mind*' is an essential book that guides readers through the process of achieving inner and outer resolutions. The concept of *Redikall Consciousness* emphasizes the connection between the subconscious mind, the body, and the soul.

Access Bars involve gently touching 32 points on the head, clearing out old mental patterns and limiting beliefs, allowing greater awareness to flow. The questioning process of Access Consciousness is a way to open the mind by shifting perspectives and inviting new possibilities. Instead of seeking definitive answers, it encourages curiosity and exploration, allowing you to break free from limitations and fixed beliefs. By asking expansive questions like *"What else is possible?"* or *"How does it get any better than this?"*, you create space for greater awareness, new opportunities, and transformation.

These practices help you release the old and open up to new levels of consciousness.

Conclusion

Expanding awareness is a journey of self-discovery and awakening. By practicing mindfulness, engaging in self-inquiry, experiencing new things, and using tools like breathwork, visualization, and energy healing, you can unlock deeper levels of consciousness. It's not about perfection, but about being open to the infinite possibilities of growth and transformation that are available to you at every moment.

Chapter 8

Truth 8: The Heart Guides You Toward Authenticity

Living authentically isn't just a trendy phrase; it's the key to living a fulfilled and aligned life. The truth is, we all have an inner compass—an intuitive guide within us that knows exactly who we are, what we truly want, and how we want to show up in the world. This compass is the heart. Yet, so often, we find ourselves living according to expectations—either our own or those imposed by society, family, or peers. We wear masks to fit in, hide our vulnerabilities, and suppress our true desires.

But the heart, with its quiet and consistent whispers, is always guiding us back to our authentic selves, the essence of who we were before we were shaped by the world around us. It invites us to shed those layers of conditioning and reconnect with the core of who we are. The more we listen to it, the easier it becomes to live authentically and make choices that are in alignment with our truth.

1. The Heart Knows Your Truth

Have you ever had that feeling where something just *feels right* or, conversely, something feels off, even if you can't explain why? That's the heart's guidance in action. The heart doesn't lie or conform to outside pressures. It simply knows your deepest desires, your values, and your purpose.

When we're truly connected to the heart, we know when we're on the right path, even if it's challenging or different from what others might expect. Authenticity doesn't mean being perfect or having everything figured out—it means being true to who you are in the moment, regardless of external opinions or societal norms.

Reflection Question:
When was the last time you felt completely aligned with your heart? What were you doing, and how did it feel? Now, consider: What would it look like if you embraced more of this alignment in your daily life?

2. Breaking Free from Societal Expectations

Living authentically requires bravery, and the first step is realizing how often we allow societal expectations to dictate our choices. From the career we choose to the way we dress and the relationships we form, so much of what we do is influenced by what others think or by cultural norms. But living authentically is about stepping away from these expectations and listening to what our heart truly desires.

The heart's voice isn't loud or forceful; it speaks in a quiet, gentle manner, urging us to honor our unique path. It invites us to redefine success on our terms, without comparing ourselves to others. It reminds us that happiness comes from being who we are, not from fitting into a mold.

Personal Insight:
Think about the societal expectations you have internalized—whether it's about success, relationships, or how you should look or behave. How do these expectations make you feel? Do they align with your true

desires? When you think about living authentically, what would your life look like if you let go of these external pressures?

3. Trusting Your Heart Over the Mind

The mind often tries to protect us by creating narratives, worrying about what could go wrong, and focusing on fear. The heart, however, is always rooted in truth, even when the mind is clouded with doubt. The challenge comes in learning to trust the heart's guidance over the mind's fear-based chatter.

The heart's wisdom often feels more peaceful and calming, even in moments of uncertainty. When we trust our hearts, we make decisions from a place of alignment, rather than fear or societal pressure. This is where true freedom lies—when we release the need to control every aspect of our lives and trust the flow of the heart.

Practice:
Try making a decision using the heart's wisdom over your mind's logic. Before making a choice, take a moment to pause, close your eyes, and tune in. Ask your heart,

"What does my soul want here?" Feel the response. Does it feel expansive and peaceful? Or does it feel tight and constricting? Trust the expansive feeling.

4. Embracing Vulnerability: The Path to Authentic Connection

Authenticity requires us to show up as we are—imperfections, flaws, and all. And part of living authentically is embracing vulnerability. The heart invites us to let down our walls, to stop pretending we are something we're not, and to open ourselves up to real connection.

When we are vulnerable, we allow ourselves to be seen for who we truly are, and that's when the magic happens. Authenticity invites deep connection with others because, when we are true to ourselves, we permit others to do the same. Vulnerability fosters trust, understanding, and love.

Reflect:
How comfortable are you with being vulnerable? Are there areas of your life where you feel you need to hide your true

self? What might happen if you allowed yourself to be more open and authentic with others?

5. Following Your Heart's Desires

The heart doesn't always take the logical path—it takes the one that feels right, that ignites passion and excitement. It is deeply connected to our desires, and when we follow our heart's desires, we align ourselves with what brings us true joy. Often, living authentically means permitting yourself to follow your heart, even if it means stepping into the unknown.

Authenticity isn't always the easiest route— it requires courage to step outside of the comfort zone and pursue what feels meaningful, even if it doesn't make sense on paper. But the heart's wisdom knows that fulfillment is found in following the desires that light us up from within.

Exercise:
Think about a desire or dream that you've tucked away because it felt unrealistic or impractical. What would it take to allow yourself to start exploring it? Even if it's just

one small step, what does your heart want you to try?

6. Trusting Your Timing

Authenticity means living at your own pace. Society often pressures us to do things by a certain age, achieve milestones by specific dates, or meet expectations that have no relevance to who we truly are. Your heart understands that timing is unique to you. There's no need to rush. When we trust our timing, we release the stress and pressure of "keeping up" with others, and we allow ourselves to flow in our rhythm.

This means trusting that everything is unfolding as it should and having patience with ourselves along the journey. The heart knows that we are always in the right place at the right time, even if the external world doesn't always agree.

Reflection:
Where in your life do you feel you are rushing or comparing yourself to others? What would it feel like to trust your timing, letting go of the need to follow a predetermined schedule?

Conclusion: Living Your Heart's Truth

Living authentically means honoring your heart, trusting its wisdom, and releasing the need to conform to societal expectations. It requires courage, vulnerability, and a deep commitment to following your path, even when it's not the easiest or most comfortable. When you allow your heart to guide you, you align with your true essence and create a life filled with meaning, joy, and fulfillment.

So, ask yourself: What would it take for you to live more authentically today? How can you begin to honor your heart's wisdom and embrace the beauty of your unique path? Your heart is waiting to guide you — are you ready to follow?

Being True to Yourself: Exercises to Recognize Your True Desires and Align Them with Your Life Choices

Living authentically is a journey of uncovering your true desires, dreams, and values, and then aligning your daily actions with them. It's about shedding the layers of conditioning, expectations, and fears that have shaped who you think you are, and reconnecting with the real you—the one that knows exactly what you want and need to thrive. The heart holds this wisdom, and through simple, heart-centered exercises, you can start to tune in and live more authentically.

Let's explore some exercises that can help you recognize your true desires and align them with your life choices.

1. Journaling to Uncover Your True Desires

Journaling is one of the most powerful ways to tap into your heart's wisdom and discover what you truly want in life. By writing freely, without judgment, you allow your subconscious mind to surface your deepest desires and unspoken truths.

Exercise: "The Heart's Whisper" Journal Prompt
Take a moment to breathe deeply and connect with your heart. Imagine you're sitting next to your heart, and it has something important to tell you. Write down whatever comes up, without

overthinking or editing. Let the words flow freely.

Prompts:

What do I truly want in my life, right now?

What brings me joy and fulfillment that I haven't allowed myself to experience fully?

If I weren't afraid of what others think, what would I do differently?

You can revisit these journal entries over time to see how your desires evolve and shift, giving you insight into your heart's authentic path.

2. Affirmations for Authentic Living

Affirmations are a wonderful tool for reprogramming the subconscious mind and shifting limiting beliefs that may block you from living authentically. These affirmations will help you re-align with your true self and give you the courage to honor your desires.

Exercise: Heart-Centered Affirmations
Write down the following affirmations on a piece of paper or in a journal, and read

them aloud each day. Allow the words to sink deep into your heart.

Affirmations:

"I trust my heart's wisdom and follow my true desires."

"I release the need for external validation and embrace my authenticity."

"Every choice I make aligns with who I truly am."

"I am worthy of living the life I desire, without compromise."

"I honor the whispers of my heart, even when they challenge the norm."

Feel the power of these words as you speak them—your heart will start to resonate with them, shifting your mindset and actions toward greater authenticity.

3. Heart-Centered Decision Making

Making decisions from the heart requires tuning out external noise and tuning into your inner wisdom. Often, the mind is full of doubts, fears, and practical considerations that can cloud your judgment. The heart, on the other hand, speaks clearly through calmness, expansion, and intuition.

Exercise: The "Heart or Head" Decision-Making Tool
Next time you have to make a decision—big or small—use this simple tool to check in with your heart.

Close your eyes, take a few deep breaths, and visualize the options in front of you.

Notice how your body feels with each option. Does it feel expansive, light, and open (this is a sign of your heart's approval)? Or does it feel heavy, tight, or anxious (this is often the mind's fear or societal expectation)?

Ask yourself: *What would my heart say if I wasn't afraid of judgment? What is the most authentic choice here?*

Write down your answers and trust your body's response. The heart doesn't lie—it always guides you toward what's most aligned with your true self.

4. Living with Heart-Centered Intentions

Living authentically is not about perfection, but about having clear intentions that align with your values and desires. When you set heart-centered intentions, you create a roadmap that helps you stay true to yourself, regardless of external distractions.

Exercise: Heart-Centered Intention Setting
Take a moment to reflect on what truly matters to you. What are the core values that guide your life? What do you want to prioritize in the upcoming days, weeks, or months?

Steps:

Sit in a quiet space and close your eyes.

Ask yourself: "What does my heart want to focus on right now? What is my deepest desire?"

Write down one or two intentions that resonate with your true desires. These can be related to your relationships, career, health, or spiritual growth.

Example Intentions:

"I intend to live in alignment with my authentic self, expressing my true thoughts and feelings openly."

"I intend to make decisions from a place of love and trust, rather than fear or external pressure."

Every day, take a moment to revisit these intentions, reflecting on whether your actions are in alignment with your heart's truth. If you find that you've drifted off course, gently bring yourself back to your heart's wisdom.

5. Heart-Driven Action Steps

Living authentically means taking action that reflects your true desires, even when it's uncomfortable or uncertain. It's about showing up for yourself, taking risks, and following through on your heart's guidance.

Exercise: Heart-Driven Action Steps
Identify one area of your life where you're not currently living authentically. It could be in your job, relationships, health, or self-care routine. Now, take a small action step

that will move you closer to authenticity in that area.

Action Ideas

If you've been staying in a relationship that doesn't serve your true self, take a courageous step to express your feelings honestly.

If you've been ignoring your creative passions, schedule time to paint, write, or engage in a hobby that makes your heart sing.

If you've been working a job that doesn't align with your values, start researching new opportunities or projects that excite you.

By taking action, you're sending a message to your heart that you are committed to living authentically. Start small—each step counts.

Conclusion: Embrace the Path of Authenticity

Recognizing your true desires and aligning them with your life choices is a transformative journey. It requires introspection, self-compassion, and courage. Through journaling, affirmations, decision-making tools, and heart-driven actions, you will begin to experience the profound freedom of living authentically.

The heart knows the way—it's time to listen, trust, and allow it to guide you toward a life that reflects your truest self. What will you choose today to live more authentically?

Chapter 9

Truth 9: The Heart Holds the Blueprint of Your Purpose

Heart's Purpose as a Blueprint

Have you ever felt like something is missing, even when everything in your life seems to be going well? Have you ever wondered, "Is this truly what I'm meant to be doing? Is this the life I'm meant to live?"

Deep within your heart lies a powerful blueprint—a map of your true purpose, one that goes beyond career success, material accomplishments, or social validation. Your heart holds the key to your soul's deepest calling, a purpose that is uniquely yours. It's the guiding force that aligns your desires, dreams, and actions with who you truly are at your core.

The blueprint of your purpose isn't something you have to search for outside of yourself. It's already embedded in your being, waiting to be discovered and embraced. It is the inner knowing that guides you toward a life that feels aligned, fulfilling, and deeply meaningful.

This chapter is about uncovering that blueprint and living a life that resonates with your heart's true purpose.

1. The Heart's Purpose vs. External Expectations

Too often, we are conditioned to believe that our purpose is something tied to external measures of success—getting a certain job, earning a specific amount of money, or meeting society's expectations. While these achievements are valuable, they don't always lead to fulfillment. They don't always lead to the sense of deep, soul-level satisfaction that comes from living in alignment with your true self.

Your heart's purpose is something much deeper. It's the feeling of peace and joy that arises when you are doing what you love when you're connected to something bigger than yourself, and when you know you're making a meaningful impact in the world— whether that's in your personal life, your career, or your relationships.

Ask yourself:

What activities make me feel most alive?

When do I feel the most aligned with who I truly am?

What do I love doing that doesn't feel like "work"?

When have I felt the most deeply connected to my soul's purpose?

These are clues that your heart is providing to guide you toward your true life purpose. The heart doesn't see purpose as something you "achieve" but as something you live—a state of being in harmony with your authentic self.

2. Recognizing Your Heart's Blueprint

Your heart's blueprint isn't a static thing. It's dynamic, ever-evolving, and deeply personal. It's the essence of your soul, woven into the fabric of who you are. It's the unique combination of your talents, passions, values, and life experiences.

To recognize this blueprint, you need to tune in with an open heart and mind, allowing yourself to step beyond the limitations of your conditioning. Trust that the answers are already inside you. They've been there all along.

Exercise: Discovering Your Heart's Blueprint

Here's an exercise to help you begin uncovering your heart's purpose. Take a few moments to sit in a quiet, comfortable space, close your eyes, and connect with your heart. Take deep breaths to center yourself.

Ask yourself: *What is it that I want to contribute to the world?*

Reflect on moments when you've felt true joy or fulfillment. What were you doing? Who were you with? How did you feel in those moments?

Write down your thoughts, feelings, and insights. Don't censor yourself—just let the words flow. This is your heart speaking.

Trust what comes up. These are often the seeds of your heart's purpose, and by recognizing them, you can start aligning your life choices with these desires.

3. The Heart's Purpose Transcends Career and Achievements

Your heart's blueprint is not confined to your job title or the accolades you collect along the way. It transcends the superficial markers of success and taps into a deeper sense of fulfillment—one that's not dependent on external validation or external circumstances.

Your purpose is woven into how you show up in the world, how you serve others, how you align with your values, and how you choose to express your unique gifts. The heart's purpose is not about achieving for the sake of achievement—it's about expressing who you truly are.

Exercise: Aligning Your Life with Your Heart's Purpose

Take a moment to reflect on your current life situation—your work, relationships, and lifestyle.

Ask yourself: *Is this in alignment with my heart's purpose?*

Identify one area where you feel misaligned. What action can you take today to move closer to alignment with your heart's purpose?

It might be a small change—a conversation with a loved one, a shift in your career, or a new commitment to self-care. Whatever it is, trust that it's a step closer to the life your heart is calling you to live.

4. Trusting the Heart's Guidance

Living in alignment with your heart's blueprint requires trust—trust that your heart knows the way and that it will lead you to the right places, people, and experiences. The heart is a guide, but it requires you to listen deeply and trust the journey.

Trust doesn't always mean certainty. It means being willing to follow the heart even when the path is unclear or when you can't see the full picture. The heart often leads you in unexpected directions, and each step is part of your unique soul's evolution.

Exercise: Trusting Your Heart's Guidance

Think about a time when you followed your heart, even when logic told you otherwise. How did that decision feel? What was the outcome?

Reflect on an area in your life where you feel uncertain. Ask your heart: *What is the next step? What is the truth that I need to hear?*

Take a moment to trust that the right answers will come. Let go of needing to control the outcome, and allow the heart to guide you, step by step.

5. Living the Blueprint: Purpose in Action

Living your heart's purpose is not just a concept—it's about taking action in alignment with what feels true to you. It's about showing up every day in a way that reflects your deepest values, desires, and soul's calling.

The blueprint of your purpose is not a destination. It's a way of living. It's about embodying your truth every day, in every decision, conversation, and action you take.

Exercise: Purposeful Living

Each day, take a few moments to reflect on how your actions align with your heart's purpose. Are there any areas where you're not fully living in alignment? What small action can you take today to bring more of your heart's wisdom into the world?

This is the beginning of living your blueprint—a life of authenticity, fulfillment, and alignment with your soul's true purpose.

Conclusion: The Heart's Blueprint Unfolds

Your heart holds the blueprint to your life's deepest purpose, a purpose that is not defined by external success or achievements, but by how you live in alignment with your truest self. It's a purpose that transcends all boundaries, connecting you to a deeper sense of fulfillment and meaning.

As you continue to listen to your heart and trust its wisdom, you'll begin to unfold the life that was always meant for you. Each step you take, each action you make in alignment with your heart, brings you closer to living your soul's purpose. This is your truth. This is your path.

Discovering Life's Purpose

Your life's purpose is a unique calling—a deep, soulful desire to live authentically and contribute in ways that align with your heart's wisdom. When you are in tune with your heart, it speaks to you clearly, guiding you toward the life that feels most true to your essence. But how do you tap into this deep wisdom? How do you connect with your purpose?

Here are a few heart-centered practices to help you discover and align with your life's purpose:

Heart-Centered Meditation: Listening to Your Inner Wisdom

Find a quiet, comfortable space where you won't be disturbed. Sit or lie down in a relaxed posture. Gently close your eyes and take a deep breath in… hold it for a moment… then exhale slowly. Let yourself settle into a state of peace and presence.

Step 1: Connect with Your Heart

Place both hands over your heart. Feel the warmth of your palms as they rest on your chest. Bring your awareness to the gentle rise and fall of your breath. With each inhale, imagine golden light filling your heart space. With each exhale, release any tension, doubt, or worry.

Step 2: Breathe into Your Heart

Take a deep breath in through your nose… and exhale through your mouth. As you continue to breathe slowly and deeply, visualize your heart glowing with a warm, radiant light—soft, inviting, and full of love. Let this light expand, filling your entire body with warmth and peace.

Step 3: Ask & Listen

Gently ask yourself:
What brings me the most joy?
What truly fulfills me at the soul level?
What is my heart guiding me toward today?

Don't force an answer. Simply listen. Let the response emerge naturally—whether in the form of words, images, emotions, or just a deep sense of knowing. If your mind starts analyzing or doubting, gently return your focus to your breath and heart center.

Step 4: Embrace the Messages

Whatever arises, accept it with gratitude. Your heart speaks in subtle whispers, not in loud demands. If no answer comes right away, trust that the wisdom is unfolding within you. You may receive insights later through a dream, a conversation, or a sudden moment of clarity.

Step 5: Close with Gratitude

Take a final deep breath. Place your hands together in gratitude, thanking your heart for its wisdom. Whisper to yourself: *I honor my heart's guidance. I trust my inner wisdom.*

When you're ready, gently open your eyes and take a moment to ground yourself before returning to your day.

Affirmation: *I listen to my heart's wisdom with trust and love. My inner guidance always leads me to joy and fulfillment.*

Journaling from the Heart: A Path to Clarity and Purpose

Journaling is a powerful way to connect with your heart's wisdom. It allows you to express your deepest thoughts, emotions, and desires without judgment or limitation. When you write from your heart, you bypass the analytical mind and tap into your inner truth.

How to Begin:

Create a Sacred Space – Find a quiet, comfortable place where you can be undisturbed. Light a candle, play soft music, or hold a crystal—anything that helps you feel centered.

Set an Intention – Take a deep breath and set an intention for your journaling session. You might say, *"I allow my heart to speak freely. I am open to receiving clarity and inspiration."*

Write Freely – Let your thoughts flow without overthinking. Don't worry about grammar, structure, or making sense—just write. Trust that your heart knows what it wants to express.

Revisit & Reflect – After writing, take a moment to read what you've written. Notice any themes, emotions, or insights that arise.

Heart-Centered Journaling Prompts:

What excites me and makes me feel alive?
What challenges have I overcome that have shaped me into who I am today?
If I had no fear and nothing held me back, what would I do?
When do I feel most connected to my true self?
What activities bring me deep joy and fulfillment?
What lessons has my heart been trying to teach me?
How can I bring more love, passion, and purpose into my life?

A Simple Exercise: The Heart Whisper Letter

Write a letter from your heart to yourself. Imagine your heart is speaking directly to you with love and guidance. What would it say? What encouragement, wisdom, or reminders would it offer? Read your letter aloud and feel the love and wisdom within it.

Affirmation: *I trust the wisdom of my heart. My words flow with clarity, truth, and purpose.*

3. Gratitude & Self-Reflection

Every day, list three things that make your heart feel full. Gratitude shifts your energy, aligning you with your purpose by focusing on what truly matters. Here are some prompts

Gratitude Prompts for Different Aspects of Life

Gratitude is a powerful practice that shifts your energy, expands your heart, and aligns you with abundance. Use these prompts to explore and deepen your appreciation for various areas of your life.

1. Gratitude for Self-Growth & Inner Journey

What personal strengths am I most grateful for?

How have my past challenges shaped me into a stronger person?

What lessons has life taught me that I deeply appreciate?

What qualities do I love and admire about myself?

How has my intuition or inner wisdom guided me in the right direction?

2. Gratitude for Relationships & Love

Who in my life has been a source of love and support, and how have they impacted me?

What acts of kindness have I received that made me feel valued?

How have my friendships enriched my life?

What special moments of connection am I thankful for today?

How can I express gratitude to someone I deeply appreciate?

3. Gratitude for the Body & Health

What do I appreciate most about my body and its abilities?

How has my body supported me through my life's journey?

What foods, movements, or self-care rituals am I grateful for?

How has my breath carried me through moments of peace and stress?

What health or healing experiences am I grateful for?

4. Gratitude for Nature & Surroundings

What aspects of nature bring me the most peace and joy?

How has a specific place or environment nurtured my soul?

What sounds, smells, or sights in nature am I grateful for today?

How has the changing of seasons reflected my personal growth?

In what ways does the Earth provide abundance for me every day?

5. Gratitude for Challenges & Growth

What past struggles am I now grateful for, and why?

How have setbacks helped me gain new perspectives?

What inner strengths have emerged because of the difficulties I've faced?

What lessons did a difficult situation teach me that I now value?

How have challenges deepened my self-awareness and resilience?

6. Gratitude for Creativity & Expression

What creative outlets bring me joy and fulfillment?

How has my creativity helped me solve problems or express emotions?

What art, music, or words have inspired and uplifted me?

How has my imagination added magic to my life?

What ideas or projects am I excited and grateful to work on?

7. Gratitude for Abundance & Prosperity

What resources and opportunities have flowed into my life?

How has money or abundance shown up for me in unexpected ways?

What skills or talents have helped me create financial well-being?

How do I feel supported and provided for by The Universe?

What is one thing I have today that I once wished for?

8. Gratitude for Spirituality & Higher Guidance

How has my spiritual journey shaped my life?

What synchronicities or signs from The Universe am I thankful for?

How has meditation, prayer, or introspection brought me clarity?

What spiritual lessons have deepened my connection to myself?

What energies, deities, or guides do I feel grateful for?

9. Gratitude for the Present Moment

What small joys did I experience today?

How did I feel supported or loved in the last 24 hours?

What simple pleasure am I deeply thankful for right now?

How has today been a gift, even in the smallest way?

What made me smile or feel at peace today?

10. Gratitude for the Unknown & Future Possibilities

What exciting possibilities am I grateful for in my future?

How do I trust that life is unfolding perfectly for me?

What dreams do I hold in my heart with gratitude, even before they manifest?

How has uncertainty led me to unexpected blessings?

What potential within me am I grateful to explore?

Affirmation: *Gratitude opens my heart, expands my energy, and brings more blessings into my life.*

4. Following Intuitive Nudges

Notice when you feel pulled toward something—be it an idea, a person, or an experience. These are clues from your heart guiding you toward your purpose.

5. Service & Contribution

Ask yourself, *how can I use my talents to uplift others?* Your purpose is often intertwined with how you can make a difference in the world.

Balance your life

Using the Wheel of Life and Ikigai, you can achieve balance, purpose, and fulfillment in your personal and professional life. Let's work on it. Take your pen and journal and start doing this.

The Life Wheel - Self-Assessment Tool

The Life Wheel is a simple yet powerful tool to evaluate balance in different areas of your life. Follow the steps below:

Step 1: Rate Your Life Areas

Rate yourself on a scale of 1 (low) to 10 (high) in the following life areas:

Career & Work – Do you feel fulfilled and passionate about your work?

Finances – Are you comfortable with your financial stability and future security?

Health & Well-being – How well do you take care of your physical and mental health?

Relationships & Love – Are your relationships nurturing and fulfilling?

Family & Social Life – Do you feel connected to your family and friends?

Personal Growth & Learning – Are you continuously learning and growing?

Fun & Recreation – Do you make time for hobbies and activities that bring joy?

Spirituality & Purpose – Do you feel connected to a higher purpose or belief system?

Step 2: Draw Your Wheel (take some help of image from Google)

Draw a circle and divide it into eight sections (like a pizza).

Label each section with one of the life areas.

Plot your rating on each section and connect the dots.

Observe: Is your wheel smooth or uneven? (If it looks like a circle, then your life is balanced. Celebrate!) (if it is uneven, then it is time to reflect on yourself)

Step 3: Reflection

Which areas need more attention?

What small steps can you take to create a more balanced wheel?

What immediate actions can improve your lower-rated areas?

Discover Your Ikigai - Your Purpose in Life

Ikigai is the Japanese concept of living with purpose and fulfillment. Follow this worksheet to find yours!

Step 1: Answer the Four Key Questions

What do I love? (Passion)

List activities that bring you joy and fulfillment.

What am I good at? (Talent)

Identify your natural skills and strengths.

What does the world need? (Mission)

Think about how you can contribute and make a difference.

What can I be paid for? (Profession)

Consider ways to turn your passion and skills into sustainable income.

Step 2: Find Your Overlapping Zone

Look for the connections between your answers.

Where do your passions, skills, world needs, and income opportunities intersect?

That's your Ikigai!

Step 3: Action Plan

How can you integrate your Ikigai into daily life?

What small steps can you take to move closer to your purpose?

What limiting beliefs are holding you back, and how can you overcome them?

Use this worksheet as a guide and evolve with it.

Life is a journey of balance and purpose. When your Life Wheel is in balance and your Ikigai is clear with your purpose, you will experience true fulfillment and joy.

Conclusions

What if the greatest wisdom you seek isn't in your mind, but in your heart?

Your heart is more than just an organ—it's a powerful intelligence center that holds the key to your healing, purpose, and true fulfillment. This book explores the profound connection between the heart, mind, body, and soul, revealing how listening to your heart's whispers can transform your health, relationships, and emotional well-being.

Through deep insights, healing exercises, and self-reflection practices, you will learn how to:

✔ Heal emotional wounds and release stored pain.

✔ Align your heart's wisdom with your life's purpose.

✔ Strengthen the connection between your mind, body, and soul for holistic well-being.

Are you ready to awaken your heart's intelligence and transform your life?

Roop Lakhani

Resources & Recommended Reading

I want to offer further resources that have been instrumental in my own growth and healing process. These books and tools have enriched my understanding and deepened my connection to the wisdom of the heart, emotions, and mind. I highly recommend exploring them if you're looking to continue your exploration of self-awareness, emotional intelligence, and personal growth.

"The Biology of Belief" by Bruce Lipton – A revolutionary book on how beliefs impact our biology and how we can reprogram our cells for health and happiness.

"You Can Heal Your Life" by Louise Hay – A foundational work that teaches how to heal emotional and physical pain through positive thought and self-love.

"Redikall Crystalline Mind" – A book focused on understanding the power of our thoughts and energy, offering insights into how to clear limiting beliefs and elevate our consciousness.

"The Power of Now" by Eckhart Tolle – A transformative book on the importance of living in the present moment and accessing the peace of the present without dwelling on the past or future.

"The Heart Math Solution" by Doc Childre and Howard Martin – Offers techniques to align your heart and mind, creating harmony within the body and improving emotional resilience.

"The Four Agreements" by Don Miguel Ruiz – A guide to personal freedom, teaching the four simple agreements to create a life of peace and fulfillment.

"Daring Greatly" by Brené Brown – A powerful exploration of vulnerability and courage, emphasizing the importance of embracing our imperfections to live a wholehearted life.

"The Untethered Soul" by Michael A. Singer – A book that teaches how to free yourself from the inner chatter and attain peace and clarity by connecting with your higher self.

Tools and Practices to Explore:

Journaling – As discussed in earlier chapters, journaling is a powerful tool for reflection, self-expression, and emotional healing.

Meditation and Mindfulness Practices – These are essential in cultivating emotional intelligence and understanding the deeper messages from the heart.

HeartMath Techniques – These techniques help you align your heart and mind, reduce stress, and foster emotional resilience.

Affirmations and Positive Thinking – Integrating positive affirmations into your daily routine can rewire your mind and body for health, happiness, and success.

By engaging with these resources and practices, you can continue to deepen your connection with your heart's intelligence and embark on an ongoing journey of healing, transformation, and self-discovery.

Call to Action

Are you feeling stuck or overwhelmed by the challenges in your life? Whether you're struggling with relationships, career decisions, emotional blocks, or simply seeking clarity on your life's purpose, you're not alone. Many people experience moments of confusion and self-doubt, but the good news is that you don't have to navigate these struggles alone.

As a Tarot Coach, Healer, and Coach, I offer a safe and supportive space for you to gain insight, heal emotional wounds, and transform your life.

If you're dealing with:

Unresolved Emotional Pain: Are past experiences and unhealed wounds holding you back from living your fullest potential? Let's uncover and release the emotional baggage that's weighing you down.

Lack of Clarity in Life's Direction: Feeling unsure about your life's purpose or career path? Through tarot guidance and coaching, we can identify your strengths and map out a clear direction for success.

Relationship Challenges: Struggling to communicate with your partner or family members? Together, we can explore the root of these conflicts and create healthier dynamics.

Negative Patterns or Limiting Beliefs: Are you stuck in a cycle of self-doubt, fear, or procrastination? It's time to break free from those patterns and create new, empowering beliefs.

Stress, Anxiety, and Overwhelm: If you're feeling constantly overwhelmed, it's important to reconnect with your inner peace. Let's explore holistic healing practices that can help you feel grounded, balanced, and energized.

Now is the time to step into your true potential and embrace your life with confidence. I invite you to book a Consultation Call and take the first step toward healing, clarity, and transformation.

All my other books.

Book 1.

Wings to Freedom: Unchained from people-pleasing

Purpose: Empowering individuals to break free from limitations and embrace their true potential. Wings to Freedom offers practical guidance and inspirational stories to help you overcome obstacles, embrace your strengths, and soar toward a life of freedom and fulfillment.

Book 2.

FLY – First Love Yourself: Embrace Your Inner Love

Purpose: Cultivating self-love as the cornerstone of a fulfilling life. This book guides you through the process of developing a deep, unconditional love for yourself, setting the stage for a more content and purposeful existence.

Book 3.

Crown of Confidence: Claiming Your Self-Worth

Purpose: Building confidence and self-respect to live authentically. Crown of Confidence provides practical tools and insights to help you develop a strong sense of self-worth and project confidence in all areas of life.

Book 4.

Emotional Alchemy: Mastering the Art of Inner Harmony

Purpose: Techniques and insights for achieving emotional mastery and stability. This book offers strategies for transforming emotional challenges into sources of strength and inner peace.

Book 5.

Belief Blueprint: Rewriting Your Mind's Map

Purpose: Transforming limiting beliefs into empowering ones for personal growth. Belief Blueprint provides methods to identify and reframe limiting beliefs, enabling you to create a more empowering mindset.

Book 6.

EFT Empowerment: Scripts for Healing and Transformation

Purpose: A practical guide of EFT scripts to address various emotions and beliefs. This book includes a collection of Emotional Freedom Techniques (EFT) scripts designed to facilitate emotional healing and transformation.

Book 7.

Energy Echoes in Relation: Navigating Relationship Dynamics

Purpose: Understanding how your energy affects relationships and identifying red flags. Energy Echoes explores the interplay between personal energy and relationship dynamics, offering insights into improving and managing your interactions with others.

Book 8.

Money Currents Reality: Harnessing Energy to Transform Financial Realities

Purpose: Exploring the link between energy and financial outcomes, addressing money wounds. This book delves into how energy influences financial well-being and provides strategies for transforming money-related issues.

Book 9.

Wisdom Whispers: Insights from My Journey of Transformation

Purpose: Sharing lessons and pearls of wisdom gained from personal growth and transformation. *Wisdom Whispers* reflects on the profound insights and lessons learned throughout my journey, offering guidance and inspiration for others on their path.

All my books are very close to my heart as they all spring from my journey.

Contact me on roop@tarotfuture.com or go to my website www.rooplakhani.com or call +91 98216 12031 to order your copy of any of my books. All books will also be available on Amazon.in & Amazon. Com

Oracle Cards

NINE Oracle Cards Created by Roop Lakhani

1. Empowerment cards
2. Surrender cards
3. Forgiving cards
4. Life Insight Oracle cards
5. Increase Your Highest Potential cards
6. Self-Love Wisdom cards
7. Inner Child Wisdom cards
8. People Pleaser Wisdom cards
9. Shadow Work Wisdom cards

How These Oracle Cards Will Guide You Toward Fulfillment

These carefully crafted oracle cards are designed to provide you with daily guidance, helping you navigate through life's challenges and step into your highest potential. Each card carries a specific message that will empower, enlighten, and encourage you to take inspired action toward your goals. Here's how the cards can support you on your journey:

Empowerment Cards

This card serves as a reminder of your inner strength and ability to take control of your life. It encourages you to tap into your power, step out of fear, and embrace the opportunities before you. When drawn, it will inspire you to take action with confidence and self-belief.

Surrender Cards

The "Surrender" card invites you to release the need to control everything. It guides you to let go of resistance and trust in the flow of life. Surrendering allows you to open yourself up to the universe's guidance and wisdom, making space for new possibilities.

Forgiving Cards

Forgiveness is a powerful tool for emotional freedom. This card encourages you to heal old wounds and let go of grudges that are holding you back. By embracing forgiveness, you clear the emotional clutter and create room for peace, love, and joy to enter your life.

Life Insight Oracle Cards

Drawing this card will provide you with a deeper understanding of the current situation in your life. It offers clarity, insight, and wisdom to help you see things from a higher perspective. It helps you connect with your intuition to make decisions that align with your soul's path.

Increase Your Highest Potential Cards

This card is all about personal growth and reaching for your highest potential. It invites you to expand your consciousness, develop your talents, and step into the person you are meant to be. It reminds you that you have the power to achieve greatness by cultivating your inner gifts.

Self-love Wisdom Cards

Self-love is the foundation for everything in life. This card guides you to nurture yourself, practice compassion, and honor your needs. It will remind you of the importance of loving yourself first, which enables you to love others and attract healthy relationships.

Inner Child Wisdom Cards

The "Inner Child" card calls you to connect with the playful, creative, and innocent part of yourself. It reminds you to embrace joy, laughter, and creativity in your life, healing old emotional wounds and allowing your true self to emerge. It helps you rediscover the lighthearted nature within you.

People Pleaser Wisdom Cards

This card offers guidance for those who often put others' needs above their own. It invites you to break free from the pattern of people-pleasing and establish healthy boundaries. The message here is to

prioritize your well-being and allow
yourself to say "no" when necessary.

Shadow Work Wisdom Cards
The "Shadow Work" card speaks to the
subconscious aspects of yourself that need
healing. It encourages you to look at the
parts of you that may be hidden or
suppressed. This card offers support in
addressing fears, insecurities, and past
traumas, leading to greater self-awareness
and healing.

How These Cards Can Help You Move Forward

Each day, as you pull a card, you will
receive a message tailored to guide you
through your current experiences. The
beauty of these oracle cards is that they
reflect the wisdom that already resides
within you, helping you to make
empowered decisions, heal emotional
wounds, and align with your soul's
purpose. Whether you're seeking guidance
in love, career, or personal growth, these
cards will provide clarity and support,

helping you move toward a life filled with fulfillment, peace, and joy.

Incorporate them into your daily routine and watch how each card's message helps you unlock deeper layers of self-awareness, healing, and empowerment. Trust the process, as the guidance you need is always within reach!

About the Author:

I, Roop am a Tarot coach, mindset healer, and transformation catalyst who has dedicated my life to helping people reconnect with their inner wisdom. With years of experience in energy healing, mindset coaching, and spiritual growth, I empower individuals to live from their heart's truth and create a life filled with love, clarity, and abundance.

As I come to the close of this journey, I reflect on the essence of what this book has meant to me. It has been more than just words on paper—it has been an exploration of the heart's intelligence, a deep dive into the emotional and spiritual realms that guide our lives. Every chapter has been an invitation to connect more deeply with our true selves, to heal old wounds, and to embrace the wisdom that resides within our hearts.

The key takeaways from this book are simple yet profound:

Heart-centered living is the key to healing, growth, and fulfillment. By tuning into the whispers of our hearts, we open ourselves to a life of purpose and joy.

Emotional intelligence allows us to understand and heal from the wounds that have shaped us. Through self-reflection, we can gain insight into our triggers and reactions, ultimately using them as tools for transformation.

Healing is a lifelong journey. It requires courage, patience, and a willingness to face the challenges head-on. But with each step, we uncover more of who we truly are and become more aligned with our soul's purpose.

I hope this book has inspired you to take a step back, to listen to your heart, and to begin your journey of healing and self-discovery. You have the power to create a life that is aligned with your highest self, and the wisdom to navigate it is already within you.

Thank you for allowing me to share this part of my heart with you. I look forward to hearing how it has touched your life, and I hope it serves as a guiding light on your path.

Website: www.rooplakhani.com
Email: roop@tarotfuture.com

Mobile: +91 98216 12031

Made in the USA
Las Vegas, NV
23 April 2025

21266266R00174